TEACHER'S PET PUBLICATIONS

LITPLAN TEACHER PACK
for
The Great Gatsby
based on the book by
F. Scott Fitzgerald

Written by
Mary B. Collins

© 1996 Teacher's Pet Publications
All Rights Reserved

This **LitPlan** for F. Scott Fitzgerald's
The Great Gatsby
has been brought to you by Teacher's Pet Publications, Inc.

Copyright Teacher's Pet Publications 1996
11504 Hammock Point
Berlin MD 21811

Only the student materials in this unit plan
such as worksheets, study questions, assignment sheets, and tests
may be reproduced multiple times for use in the purchaser's classroom.

For any additional copyright questions,
contact Teacher's Pet Publications.

www.tpet.com

TABLE OF CONTENTS - *The Great Gatsby*

Introduction	5
Unit Objectives	7
Reading Assignment Sheet	8
Unit Outline	9
Study Questions (Short Answer)	13
Quiz/Study Questions (Multiple Choice)	22
Pre-reading Vocabulary Worksheets	37
Lesson One (Introductory Lesson)	49
Nonfiction Assignment Sheet	51
Oral Reading Evaluation Form	53
Writing Assignment 1	56
Writing Assignment 2	60
Writing Assignment 3	73
Writing Evaluation Form	58
Vocabulary Review Activities	61
Extra Writing Assignments/Discussion ?s	64
Unit Review Activities	74
Unit Tests	77
Unit Resource Materials	107
Vocabulary Resource Materials	121

A FEW NOTES ABOUT THE AUTHOR
F. SCOTT FITZGERALD

FITZGERALD, F. Scott (1896-1940). The novels and short stories of F. Scott Fitzgerald are famous for portraying the "lost generation" of the post-World War I era. They depict the rich disenchanted youth of what he called the Jazz Age.

Francis Scott Key Fitzgerald was born in St. Paul, Minn., on Sept. 24, 1896, the only son of Edward and Mary Fitzgerald. His father was a descendant of Francis Scott Key, author of 'The Star-Spangled Banner'. Fitzgerald attended St. Paul Academy and the Newman School, in New Jersey. After entering Princeton University in 1913 he wrote for student publications. In November 1917 Fitzgerald left college to enlist in the Army. While stationed in Montgomery, Ala., he fell in love with Zelda Sayre.

Following his release from the Army in 1919, Fitzgerald worked for an advertising agency in New York City for several months. After Zelda broke their engagement, he returned to St. Paul to rewrite a novel he had worked on when he was in the Army. The novel-'This Side of Paradise'-was published in 1920. The first chronicle of flaming youth, it brought Fitzgerald fame, money, and marriage to Zelda. The couple had one daughter. To maintain the luxurious life he and his wife liked to lead, Fitzgerald wrote at a furious pace. In 1920 he published 'Flappers and Philosophers', a volume of short stories. His second novel, 'The Beautiful and Damned', and 'Tales of the Jazz Age' appeared in 1922. In 1924 the Fitzgeralds moved to Europe, where Fitzgerald wrote his masterpiece, 'The Great Gatsby'. Typical of his work, it glorified romance and disillusionment, and the dialogue was flawless.

In 1930 Zelda suffered a breakdown, a step on the way to her insanity. The family returned to the United States in 1930. Fitzgerald's novel 'Tender Is the Night' was published in 1934. It failed to sell, and Fitzgerald felt defeated. In 1936 he wrote about his emotional state in 'The Crack-up'. Fitzgerald went to Hollywood in 1937 to write scenarios for motion pictures. On Dec. 20, 1940, he suffered a fatal heart attack. He had begun a novel about Hollywood, called 'The Last Tycoon'. The unfinished work, published in 1941, was another attempt to create his dream of the promises of American life and of a man who could realize them.

-- Courtesy of Compton's Learning Company

INTRODUCTION - *The Great Gatsby*

This unit has been designed to develop students' reading, writing, thinking, and language skills through exercises and activities related to *The Great Gatsby* by F. Scott Fitzgerald. It includes twenty lessons, supported by extra resource materials.

The **introductory lesson** introduces students to some background to the novel through a film (teacher supplied). Following the introductory activity, students are given a transition to explain how the activity relates to the book they are about to read. Following the transition, students are given the materials they will be using during the unit. At the end of the lesson, students begin the pre-reading work for the first reading assignment.

The **reading assignments** are approximately thirty pages each; some are a little shorter while others are a little longer. Students have approximately 15 minutes of pre-reading work to do prior to each reading assignment. This pre-reading work involves reviewing the study questions for the assignment and doing some vocabulary work for 8 to 10 vocabulary words they will encounter in their reading.

The **study guide questions** are fact-based questions; students can find the answers to these questions right in the text. These questions come in two formats: short answer required or multiple choice. The best use of these materials is probably to use the short answer version of the questions as study guides for students (since answers will be more complete), and to use the multiple choice version for occasional quizzes. If your school has the appropriate equipment, it might be a good idea to make transparencies of your answer keys for the overhead projector.

The **vocabulary work** is intended to enrich students' vocabularies as well as to aid in the students' understanding of the book. Prior to each reading assignment, students will complete a two-part worksheet for approximately 8 to 10 vocabulary words in the upcoming reading assignment. Part I focuses on students' use of general knowledge and contextual clues by giving the sentence in which the word appears in the text. Students are then to write down what they think the words mean based on the words' usage. Part II nails down the definitions of the words by giving students dictionary definitions of the words and having students match the words to the correct definitions based on the words' contextual usage. Students should then have a good understanding of the words when they meet them in the text.

After each reading assignment, students will go back and formulate answers for the study guide questions. Discussion of these questions serves as a **review** of the most important events and ideas presented in the reading assignments.

After students complete reading the work, there is a **vocabulary review** lesson which pulls together all of the fragmented vocabulary lists for the reading assignments and gives students a review of all of the words they have studied.

A lesson is devoted to the **extra discussion questions/writing assignments**. These questions focus on interpretation, critical analysis and personal response, employing a variety of thinking skills and adding to the students' understanding of the novel.

There are two **group activities** students working in small groups to discuss symbolism and characterization in the novel.

The group activity is followed by a **reports and discussion** session in which the groups share their ideas about the themes with the entire class; thus, the entire class is exposed to information about all of the themes and the entire class can discuss each theme based on the nucleus of information brought forth by each of the groups.

There are three **writing assignments** in this unit, each with the purpose of informing, persuading, or having students express personal opinions. The first assignment is to inform: students explain how the houses of the main characters are appropriate for their social position and personalities. The second assignment is to persuade: students choose from one of three persuasive letters to write. The third assignment is to give students a chance to express their own opinions and to think about their own futures: they write out a plan for their own success.

In addition, there is a **nonfiction reading assignment**. Students are required to read a piece of nonfiction related in some way to *The Great Gatsby*. After reading their nonfiction pieces, students will fill out a worksheet on which they answer questions regarding facts, interpretation, criticism, and personal opinions. During one class period, students make **oral presentations** about the nonfiction pieces they have read. This not only exposes all students to a wealth of information, it also gives students the opportunity to practice **public speaking**.

The **review lesson** pulls together all of the aspects of the unit. The teacher is given four or five choices of activities or games to use which all serve the same basic function of reviewing all of the information presented in the unit.

The **unit test** comes in two formats: multiple choice or short answer. As a convenience, two different tests for each format have been included. There is also an advanced short answer test for students who need more of a challenge.

There are additional **support materials** included with this unit. The **extra activities packet** includes suggestions for an in-class library, crossword and word search puzzles related to the novel, and extra vocabulary worksheets. There is a list of **bulletin board ideas** which gives the teacher suggestions for bulletin boards to go along with this unit. In addition, there is a list of **extra class activities** the teacher could choose from to enhance the unit or as a substitution for an exercise the teacher might feel is inappropriate for his/her class. **Answer keys** are located directly after the **reproducible student materials** throughout the unit. The student materials may be reproduced for use in the teacher's classroom without infringement of copyrights.

UNIT OBJECTIVES - *The Great Gatsby*

1. To expose students to a different era of American life.

2. Students will demonstrate their understanding of the text on four levels: factual, interpretive, critical and personal.

3. Students will consider what it means to be successful and/or rich, and the responsibilities that accompany success and/or wealth.

4. Students will be given the opportunity to practice reading aloud and silently to improve their skills in each area.

5. Students will answer questions to demonstrate their knowledge and understanding of the main events and characters in *The Great Gatsby* as they relate to the author's theme development.

6. Students will enrich their vocabularies and improve their understanding of the novel through the vocabulary lessons prepared for use in conjunction with the novel.

7. The writing assignments in this unit are geared to several purposes:
    a. To have students demonstrate their abilities to inform, to persuade, or to express their own personal ideas

    > Note: Students will demonstrate ability to write effectively to <u>inform</u> by developing and organizing facts to convey information. Students will demonstrate the ability to write effectively to <u>persuade</u> by selecting and organizing relevant information, establishing an argumentative purpose, and by designing an appropriate strategy for an identified audience. Students will demonstrate the ability to write effectively to <u>express personal ideas</u> by selecting a form and its appropriate elements.

    b. To check the students' reading comprehension
    c. To make students think about the ideas presented by the novel
    d. To encourage logical thinking
    e. To provide an opportunity to practice good grammar and improve students' use of the English language.

8. Students will read aloud, report, and participate in large and small group discussions to improve their public speaking and personal interaction skills.

READING ASSIGNMENT SHEET - *The Great Gatsby*

Date Assigned	Reading Assignment	Completion Date
	1 - 2	
	3	
	4 - 5	
	6 - 7	
	8 - 9	

UNIT OUTLINE - *The Great Gatsby*

1 Introduction P & V 1-2	2 Read 1-2 Orally	3 ?s 1-2 P & V 3 Read 3	4 Quiz/?s P & V 4-5 Read 4-5	5 ?s 4-5 Writing Assignment 1
6 P & V 6&7 Read 6&7	7 ?s 6&7 PV&R 8-9 Writing Conf.	8 ?s 8-9 Group Activity	9 Writing Assignment 2	10 Vocabulary
11 Group Activity	12 Reports & Discussion	13 Extra ?s & Quotes	14 Library Planning Session	15 Planning
16 Nonfiction	17 Writing Assignment 3	18 20's Day	19 Review	20 Test

KEY: P = preview study   ?s   V = vocabulary work   R = read

STUDY GUIDE QUESTIONS

SHORT ANSWER STUDY GUIDE QUESTIONS - *The Great Gatsby*

Chapter 1
1. How does the narrator describe Gatsby?
2. From where did the narrator come and why?
3. Describe the narrator's house.
4. Describe the Buchanans' house.
5. How does Nick know Daisy and Tom?
6. Describe Tom. What is our impression of him in Chapter 1?
7. What kind of person is Daisy?
8. What did Miss Baker tell Nick about Tom?
9. When asked about her daughter, what does Daisy say?
10. How is Gatsby introduced into the novel?

Chapter 2
1. What is the "valley of ashes"?
2. What are the "eyes of Dr. T. J. Eckleburg?
3. Who did Tom take Nick to meet?
4. Identify Myrtle and George Wilson.
5. What did Mrs. Wilson buy while she was out with Tom and Nick?
6. Where did they go? What was at 158th Street?
7. Identify Catherine and Mr. & Mrs. McKee.
8. What does Mr. McKee tell Nick about Gatsby?
9. What reason did Myrtle give for marrying George Wilson?
10. What did Tom do to Myrtle when she mentioned Daisy's name?

Chapter 3
1. Describe Gatsby's wealth. List some of the things that represent wealth.
2. What kind of people come to Gatsby's parties?
3. Why did Nick Carraway go to the party?
4. How does Nick meet Gatsby?
5. What are some of the stories about Gatsby?
6. Is Gatsby a "phony"?
7. Describe Nick's relationship with Jordan.

Chapter 4
1. Who is Klipspringer?
2. What does Gatsby tell Nick about himself?
3. What "matter" did Gatsby have Jordan Baker discuss with Nick?
4. Who is Mr. Wolfshiem?
5. What does Mr. Wolfshiem tell Nick about Gatsby?
6. What does Jordan tell Nick about Daisy, Gatsby and Tom?

Gatsby Short Answer Study Guide Page 2

Chapter 5
1. Describe the meeting between Gatsby and Daisy. Why was he so nervous?
2. How long did it take Gatsby to make the money to buy the mansion?
3. Why did Gatsby want Daisy to see the house and his clothes?
4. What had the green light on the dock meant to Gatsby?
5. What had Gatsby turned Daisy into in his own mind?

Chapter 6
1. What is Gatsby's real history? Where is he from, and what is his name?
2. What did Dan Cody do for Gatsby?
3. What is Daisy's opinion of Gatsby's party? How does this affect him?
4. What does Gatsby want from Daisy?

Chapter 7
1. What was Gatsby's reaction to Daisy's child?
2. What did Wilson do to Myrtle? Why?
3. Why do the five drive into the city on such a hot afternoon?
4. What does Gatsby think about Daisy's relationship with Tom?
5. What is Daisy's reaction to both men?
6. What happens on the way home from New York?
7. How do these people react to Myrtle's death:
    a. Wilson:
    b. Tom:
    c. Nick:
    d. Gatsby:
8. What is the true relationship between Daisy and Tom?

Chapter 8
1. What does Gatsby tell Nick about his past? Is it true?
2. What does Michaelis believe caused Myrtle to run?
3. Why did she run?
4. Why does Wilson believe that Gatsby killed Myrtle?
5. What does Wilson do?

Chapter 9
1. Why couldn't Nick get anyone to come to Gatsby's funeral?
2. Who is Henry C. Gatz?
3. What is the book Henry Gatz shows Nick? Why is it important to the novel?
4. What happens between Nick and Jordan Baker?
5. What does Nick say about people like Daisy and Tom?

ANSWER KEY: STUDY GUIDE QUESTIONS - *The Great Gatsby*

Chapter 1

1. How does the narrator describe Gatsby?
    He says Gatsby had an extraordinary gift for hope, a romantic readiness such as he had never found in another person.

2. From where did the narrator come and why?
    The narrator came from the Midwest to study the bond business.

3. Describe the narrator's house.
    The house is very average, middle-class. It is nothing extraordinary like his neighbors' houses. It is small and sort-of stuck in between the mansions, as if it had been overlooked.

4. Describe the Buchanans' house.
    The Buchanans have a Colonial Georgian mansion. It is very formal and traditional.

5. How does Nick know Daisy and Tom?
    Daisy is Nick's cousin, and he knew Tom from his school years.

6. Describe Tom. What is our impression of him in Chapter 1?
    Tom has an athletic build and an arrogant attitude. He is an old-money snob.

7. What kind of person is Daisy?
    In this chapter, we see Daisy as a flighty socialite--very superficial.

8. What did Miss Baker tell Nick about Tom?
    She told him that Tom had a mistress. It is interesting to note that she thought "everyone" knew about Tom's mistress, and yet she whispers a "family secret" about the butler's nose.

9. When asked about her daughter, what does Daisy say?
    Daisy says, "I'm glad it's a girl. And I hope she'll be a fool–that's the best thing a girl can be in this world, a beautiful little fool."

10. How is Gatsby introduced into the novel?
    His name first comes up in conversation between Nick and Jordan. Later, Nick sees him out on the lawn in the moonlight, but Gatsby quickly vanishes. These first appearances help introduce Gatsby's mysteriousness.

Chapter 2

1. What is the "valley of ashes"?
    The valley of ashes is an industrial zone on the way to the city. It sharply contrasts with the wealthy neighborhoods of Gatsby and the Buchanans.

2. What are the "eyes of Dr. T. J. Eckleburg?
   They are on a billboard, apparently close to George B. Wilson's garage, near the valley of ashes.

3. Who did Tom take Nick to meet?
   Tom took Nick to meet his mistress.

4. Identify Myrtle and George Wilson.
   Myrtle Wilson was Tom's mistress. George was her husband, who, we learn later, kills Gatsby and himself.

5. What did Mrs. Wilson buy while she was out with Tom and Nick?
   She bought a dog.

6. Where did they go? What was at 158th Street?
   They went to an apartment that Tom apparently kept for their meetings.

7. Identify Catherine and Mr. & Mrs. McKee.
   Catherine is Myrtle's sister. Mr. and Mrs. McKee live downstairs at the apartment complex.

8. What does Catherine tell Nick about Gatsby?
   She tells Nick that Gatsby is the nephew of Kaiser Wilhelm, another rumor which adds to Gatsby's mysteriousness.

9. What reason did Myrtle give for marrying George Wilson?
   She thought he was a gentleman, but she regretted marrying him when she found out he borrowed a suit from a friend to wear to the wedding.

10. What did Tom do to Myrtle when she mentioned Daisy's name?
    He hit her and broke her nose.

Chapter 3

1. Describe Gatsby's wealth. List some of the things that represent wealth.
   Gatsby's wealth is "new" money; recently acquired, not old, family money. He is one of the newly rich in the post-war period of the twenties. He spends his money on flashy, extravagant things (a huge home, a fantastic car, and wild parties).

2. What kind of people come to Gatsby's parties?
   The newly-rich, famous, and their friends came to Gatsby's parties.

3. Why did Nick Carraway go to the party?
   Nick went because Gatsby sent him a direct invitation, and he was curious about his neighbor.

4. How does Nick meet Gatsby?
   He casually starts a conversation and Nick doesn't realize he is talking to Gatsby until Nick asks where Gatsby is.

5. What are some of the stories about Gatsby?
   Some said he killed a man; some said he was a German spy during the war.

6. Is Gatsby a "phony"?
   Yes, in the strictest sense of the word, but his motivating ideal is somewhat redeeming.

7. Describe Nick's relationship with Jordan.
   They are just starting to be friendly and a romantic interest is building.

Chapter 4
1. Who is Klipspringer?
   He is "the boarder," someone who always seems to be at Gatsby's house.

2. What does Gatsby tell Nick about himself?
   Gatsby tells Nick that he was educated at Oxford, his family died, he came into some money, and when the war came, he got some medals. He showed Nick the medals and a picture of himself with his college mates.

3. What "matter" did Gatsby have Jordan Baker discuss with Nick?
   Jordan discussed Nick's arranging a luncheon meeting between himself and Daisy at Nick's house.

4. Who is Mr. Wolfshiem?
   He is a business associate of Gatsby. Actually he is a racketeer and a very shady character. He fixed the World Series of 1919.

5. What does Mr. Wolfshiem tell Nick about Gatsby?
   He said that Gatsby was the kind of man you'd like to take home and introduce to your mother and your sister.

6. What does Jordan tell Nick about Daisy, Gatsby and Tom?
   She tells him that Daisy and Gatsby had a romance. Rumor had it that she tried to see Gatsby off to war, but her family would not let her go. Soon after, she married Tom. They seemed to be happy and then Tom had a mistress.

Chapter 5
1. Describe the meeting between Gatsby and Daisy. Why was he so nervous?
> The meeting was, at first, very awkward. Gatsby was nervous because his dream was on the threshold of coming true (or not). After they had a chance to talk, they were more at ease, and we presume rekindled their romance.

2. How long did it take Gatsby to make the money to buy the mansion?
> It took him three years.

3. Why did Gatsby want Daisy to see the house and his clothes?
> He wanted to impress her with his wealth and to show her that he could afford to take care of her in the style to which she had been accustomed.

4. What had the green light on the dock meant to Gatsby?
> It stood for his vision of his future with Daisy.

5. What had Gatsby turned Daisy into in his own mind?
> She was a larger-than-life person. "The vitality of his illusion had gone beyond Daisy – beyond everything."

Chapter 6
1. What is Gatsby's real history? Where is he from, and what is his name?
> He is James Gatz from North Dakota.

2. What did Dan Cody do for Gatsby?
> Gatsby changed his name at age 17 when he met Dan Cody. Gatsby left to travel with Cody, which he did until Cody died. He inherited a large sum of Cody's money, but never got it because of legal technicalities. Cody educated Gatsby about money and the people who have it.

3. What is Daisy's opinion of Gatsby's party? How does this affect him?
> Daisy does not like Gatsby's party. It is too much like an amusement park. When Gatsby figures out what she thinks, it disheartens him.

4. What does Gatsby want from Daisy?
> He wants her to admit that she never loved Tom, that she always did and does still love Gatsby, and he wants her to leave Tom for him.

Chapter 7
1. What was Gatsby's reaction to Daisy's child?
> He looks at her with surprise.

2. What did Wilson do to Myrtle? Why?
   Wilson locked Myrtle in her room until they are able to get away from the area. He suspects she is having an affair.

3. Why do the four drive into the city on such a hot afternoon?
   Daisy says, "It's so hot and everything's so confused. Let's go to town." She wants to change the subject and not have a confrontation between Tom and Gatsby, but more than that, the city represents a place where one can get away from personal problems by being swept away by the busy, exciting city life.

4. What does Gatsby think about Daisy's relationship with Tom?
   He truly believes that she never did love him.

5. What is Daisy's reaction to both men?
   She is obviously torn. She wants the escape that Gatsby provides, but she recognizes that a permanent relationship with him would not work. She needs Tom, who is just as superficial and "careless" as she is. She also agrees with the one who bullies her the most, Tom.

6. What happens on the way home from New York?
   Gatsby and Daisy are driving home together in Gatsby's car. Daisy is driving to help calm herself after the confrontation between the two men. At Wilson's place, Myrtle runs out into the road. Daisy runs into her with Gatsby's car, sees that she has been hit, but instead of stopping at the accident, continues home.

7. How do these people react to Myrtle's death:
   a. Wilson: feels guilty as though he is responsible for her having the affair (and therefore for her running out into the road to her new man)
   b. Tom: His first instinct is to protect himself by telling Wilson that the yellow car was not his. He orders people around at the scene (as usual). Then he cried on the way home.
   c. Nick: He felt sick and wanted to be left alone. He obviously felt bad about Myrtle and for George. He was worried about Gatsby and Daisy, and he was mad at Jordan for inviting him in to dinner.
   d. Gatsby: Gatsby's main concern was for Daisy. He thought of little else and did not want to hear the details of the accident scene.

8. What is the true relationship between Daisy and Tom?
   They are birds of a feather. Daisy is a fairly weak person and Tom is very domineering, but they are both "careless" people. Neither one takes responsibility for his own actions.

Chapter 8

1. What does Gatsby tell Nick about his past? Is it true?
   He says he met Daisy and fell in love with her. He pretended to be able to take care of her, but he couldn't. She loved him, too, at that time. He went to the war and then to Oxford. Daisy wanted him to come home, but he couldn't or wouldn't. Daisy, under pressure to marry well, married Tom. Yes, it is true in basic facts.

2. What does Michaelis believe caused Myrtle to run?
   He thinks she was running away from Wilson.

3. Why did she run?
   She thought Tom was in the yellow car because she had seen him in it earlier. She was running towards Tom.

4. Why does Wilson believe that Gatsby killed Myrtle?
   Tom told him that the yellow car was Gatsby's.

5. What does Wilson do?
   Wilson kills Gatsby and himself.

Chapter 9

1. Why couldn't Nick get anyone to come to Gatsby's funeral?
   Gatsby had no close friends. All of the party people were too shallow to hardly even meet him, much less become friends or care enough to attend his funeral. Tom and Daisy had gone out of town. Wolfshiem was so shady he couldn't be seen at a funeral of someone who had been murdered. Klipspringer is more concerned about getting his gym shoes back than Gatsby's death.

2. Who is Henry C. Gatz?
   He is Gatsby's father.

3. What is the book Henry Gatz shows Nick? Why is it important to the novel?
   It is a copy of *Hopalong Cassidy* with one of Gatsby's personal schedules in it. It shows Gatsby's planning, his desire to work to get ahead, and his spirit for romantic adventure. All of these characteristics are classically American characteristics, which on a symbolic level lift Gatsby from being just another character to representing the good ol' American spirit.

4. What happens between Nick and Jordan Baker?
   Nick breaks off the relationship. He just can't stand the ease with which she (and Tom and Daisy) let things slip by. They are too irresponsible for his moral sensibilities.

5. What does Nick say about people like Daisy and Tom?
    He says they were careless -- they smashed up things and creatures and retreated back to whatever kept them together, and they let other people clean up the mess they had made.

MULTIPLE CHOICE STUDY GUIDE/QUIZ QUESTIONS - *The Great Gatsby*

Chapter 1

1. How does the narrator describe Gatsby?
    a. Gatsby was brilliant, although somewhat smug and self-centered.
    b. Gatsby had an extraordinary gift for hope, and a romantic readiness.
    c. Gatsby was a big, hulking brute of a man.
    d. Gatsby was self-assured and showed boundless enthusiasm about most topics.

2. From where did the narrator come and why?
    a. From France to establish a vineyard in New York
    b. From the south to become an actor on Broadway
    c. From the northwest to be a fashion designer
    d. From the Midwest to study the bond business

3. Describe the narrator's house.
    a. It is one of the largest on the island, made of brick and surrounded by gardens.
    b. It is a renovated carriage house on the grounds of one of the mansions.
    c. It is a weatherbeaten bungalow squeezed between the mansions.
    d. It is roomy, but not too large for one person, with a gazebo and a boathouse.

4. Describe the Buchanan's house.
    a. It is a formal and traditional colonial Georgian mansion.
    b. It is low and modernistic, designed to blend in with the scenery.
    c. It is a replica of a Spanish hacienda, with a central garden and fountains.
    d. It is palatial, although in a state of disrepair.

5. How does Nick know Daisy and Tom?
    a. Nick and Tom served in the war together. He met Daisy at their wedding.
    b. Nick and Daisy went to school together. Daisy was dating Tom.
    c. He met them through a friend of his parents in Chicago.
    d. Daisy and Nick are cousins. Nick and Tom knew each other from school.

6. Describe Tom. What is our impression of him in Chapter 1?
    a. He is short and fat and jolly.
    b. He has an athletic build and an arrogant attitude. He is an old-money snob.
    c. He is tall and slender. He is a grumpy middle-aged man.
    d. He has a medium build and is balding. He is easy-going and pleasant.

Gatsby Multiple Choice Study Questions Page 2

7. What kind of person is Daisy?
    a. Daisy is flighty and very superficial.
    b. Daisy is an intellectual.
    c. Daisy is a down-to-earth, sweet, naive young woman.
    d. Daisy is just plain mean.

8. What did Miss Baker tell Nick about Tom?
    a. Tom is terminally ill.
    b. Tom is in trouble with the police.
    c. Tom is connected with criminals.
    d. Tom is having an affair.

9. When asked about her daughter, what does Daisy say?
    a. "She acts just like her father!"
    b. "Isn't she a little darling?"
    c. "I'm glad it's a girl. And I hope she'll be a fool–that's the best thing a girl can be in this world, a beautiful little fool."
    d. "I wish I had never had her."

10. How is Gatsby introduced into the novel?
    a. He is mentioned in a conversation between Nick and Jordan. Later Nick sees him on the lawn in the moonlight.
    b. Nick meets him at a party.
    c. Everyone talks about him at the party, but no one sees him. Later Nick sees him with Daisy.
    d. Jordan tells Daisy about Tom's affair, and Daisy meets Gatsby to begin an affair of her own to get even with Tom.

Gatsby Multiple Choice Study Questions Page 3

<u>Chapter 2</u>
11. What is the "valley of ashes"?
    a. An area in East Egg where a fire had been many years ago
    b. A barren area separating East Egg from West Egg
    c. An industrial zone
    d. An imaginary place used as a metaphor for Gatsby's loneliness

12. What are the "eyes of Dr. T. J. Eckleburg?
    a. Seeing eye dogs that the doctor trains for the Association for the Blind
    b. A group of security guards who monitor the doctor's home and offices
    c. A new kind of contact lens that the doctor has just developed
    d. An illustration on a billboard

13. Who did Tom take Nick to meet?
    a. His mistress
    b. Dr. T.J. Eckleburg
    c. His parents
    d. Gatsby

14. Identify Myrtle and George Wilson.
    a. Myrtle is Tom's cousin. George is her son.
    b. George is Tom's business partner. Myrtle is his wife.
    c. Myrtle is Tom's mistress. George is her husband.
    d. They are the caretakers on Tom's estate.

15. What did Mrs. Wilson buy while she was out with Tom and Nick?
    a. Sandwiches for lunch
    b. A dog
    c. A new dress
    d. Cuff links for Tom

16. Where did they go? What was at 158th Street?
    a. Tom's favorite restaurant
    b. Nick's office
    c. The dealer where Tom bought his last car
    d. The apartment where Tom met his mistress

Gatsby Multiple Choice Study Questions Page 4

17. Identify Catherine and Mr. & Mrs. McKee.
    a. Catherine is Nick's secretary. Mrs. McKee is her sister, and Mr. McKee is her brother-in-law.
    b. Catherine is Myrtle's sister. The McKees live downstairs at the apartment complex.
    c. Catherine is Tom's cousin. The McKees are the apartment managers.
    d. Catherine is Mrs. McKee's best friend. The McKees are old neighbors of Myrtle's.

18. What does Catherine tell Nick about Gatsby?
    a. Gatsby is the son of a Texas oil tycoon.
    b. Gatsby has recently been released from a mental hospital.
    c. Gatsby donated a half-million dollars to an orphanage in his home town.
    d. Gatsby is the nephew of Kaiser Wilhelm.

19. What reason did Myrtle give for marrying George Wilson?
    a. She had to do something to get away from her abusive parents.
    b. She did it to spite George's former girlfriend.
    c. She thought he was a gentleman; later she found out differently.
    d. She didn't think she would ever find a husband, and she was grateful to him for asking her.

20. What did Tom do to Myrtle when she mentioned Daisy's name?
    a. He hit her and broke her nose.
    b. He laughed and called her a jealous fool.
    c. He taunted her and repeated Daisy's name several more times.
    d. He ignored her and went on with his conversation with Nick.

Gatsby Multiple Choice Study Questions Page 5

Chapter 3

21. Which one of these does not represent Gatsby's wealth
    a. Made in the post-war period
    b. Spending on flashy, extravagant things
    c. Old, family money
    d. Wild parties

22. What kind of people come to Gatsby's parties?
    a. The newly rich, famous, and their friends
    b. Only the residents of West Egg
    c. Scholars and intellectuals from area universities
    d. Mostly Gatsby's business associates

23. Why did Nick Carraway go to the party?
    a. He went as Jordan Baker's escort.
    b. Gatsby sent him a direct invitation.
    c. He thought he could sneak in without being noticed.
    d. Daisy and Tom dared him to go.

24. How does Nick meet Gatsby?
    a. Gatsby greets all of his guests in a receiving line.
    b. They met when Nick wandered into the library where Gatsby was reading.
    c. Jordan Baker introduced them.
    d. Nick asks a man he is talking to where Gatsby is and discovers that he is talking to Gatsby.

25. Which is not one of the stories about Gatsby?
    a. He inherited his money from his mother, a French baroness.
    b. He killed a man.
    c. He was a German spy during the war.
    d. He was in the American army during the war.

26. Which of these words describes Gatsby?
    a. Aggressive
    b. Cruel
    c. Phony
    d. Loving

27. Describe Nick's relationship with Jordan.
    a. They can't stand each other.
    b. They are beginning to get friendly.
    c. They fell in love at first sight.
    d. They are just golfing partners.

Gatsby Multiple Choice Study Questions Page 6

Chapter 4

28. Who is Klipspringer?
	a. He is the "boarder" who always seems to be at Gatsby's house.
	b. He is Gatsby's financial advisor.
	c. He is one of Gatsby's cousins from Germany.
	d. He is Gatsby's brother-in-law.

29. What does Gatsby tell Nick about himself?
	a. He had never finished high school, he was a boatswains mate during the war, and he had been married twice.
	b. He had a degree in Finance from the University of Pennsylvania, he had been draft exempt because of his vision, and he made all of his money in the theater.
	c. He dropped out of college to go into the army, he intended to be a career military man, but inherited his money from his wife when she died unexpectedly.
	d. He was educated at Oxford, inherited his money from his family, and got some medals in the war.

30. What "matter" did Gatsby have Jordan Baker discuss with Nick?
	a. Gatsby had a business deal he wanted to include Nick in on it.
	b. Gatsby wanted Nick to arrange a luncheon meeting between himself and Daisy.
	c. Gatsby had a cousin who was coming to stay for a month, and he wanted Nick to escort her around the city, if Jordan approved.
	d. Gatsby wanted to invite Nick and Jordan to go on a golfing vacation to Europe.

31. Who is Mr. Wolfshiem?
	a. He is the owner of Gatsby's favorite restaurant in New York. He secretly arranged to have a member of the mob murdered outside the restaurant.
	b. He is Jordan Baker's coach and manager. He thinks Jordan is spending too much time with Nick and not enough on her golf.
	c. He is a racketeer and a business associate of Gatsby's. He fixed the 1919 World Series.
	d. He is the president of the company where Nick is working. He wants to bring Gatsby in on a new real estate deal.

32. What does Mr. Wolfshiem tell Nick about Gatsby?
	a. Gatsby was dangerous and should never be trusted.
	b. Gatsby was on the verge of bankruptcy because of some bad investments.
	c. Gatsby was thinking of getting into politics.
	d. Gatsby was the kind of man to take home to meet your mother and sister.

33. What does Jordan tell Nick about Daisy, Gatsby and Tom?
	a. They all grew up together in Louisiana. Tom and Gatsby had been best friends until their jealousy about Daisy got between them. Tom doesn't know that Gatsby lives nearby. Gatsby wants to make sure Nick never invites Daisy and Tom to one of the parties.
	b. Gatsby knows Tom through business dealings. He met Daisy recently at a party and wanted to get to know her better.
	c. Daisy and Gatsby had had an earlier romance. Her parents wouldn't let her see him off to war. Then she married Tom, and soon found out that he had a mistress.
	d. Gatsby and Daisy have been seeing each other for a long time. Gatsby offered Tom a large sum of money to divorce Daisy, but Tom refused.

Gatsby Multiple Choice Study Questions Page 7

Chapter 5

34. Describe the meeting between Gatsby and Daisy.
    a. Daisy did not recognize him. He was embarrassed and tried to leave, but Nick stopped him.
    b. It was initially very awkward. Gatsby was nervous. They became more at ease as they talked.
    c. Daisy was upset with Nick for not warning her. She did not want to see Gatsby and left as soon as her chauffeur returned.
    d. It was love at first sight for both of them. They wandered off into the living room and left Nick alone in the kitchen.

35. How long did it take Gatsby to make the money to buy the mansion?
    a. Three years
    b. Eleven months
    c. Two hours
    d. Fifteen days

36. What did Gatsby do to impress Daisy?
    a. He gave her a pearl necklace worth $500,000.
    b. He showed her his house and elegant clothes.
    c. He took her for a ride in his hydroplane.
    d. He showed her the love letters he had written her, but never sent.

37. What had the green light on the dock meant to Gatsby?
    a. It was clear to land the hydroplane.
    b. It was safe for him and his guests to go swimming.
    c. It stood for his vision of his future with Daisy.
    d. It was a tribute to his companions who had died in the war.

38. What does this line from the book mean? "The vitality of his illusion had gone beyond Daisy-beyond everything."
    a. He was so energized he was becoming manic.
    b. The meeting was not as good as he had fantasized, and he was very disappointed.
    c. He was mentally unstable and unable to cope with reality.
    d. He had, through his years of dreaming, made her larger-than-life.

Gatsby Multiple Choice Study Questions Page 8

Chapter 6

39. What is Gatsby's real name and where is he from?
- a. He is James Gatz from North Dakota.
- b. He is Floyd Jay Geisinger from Nevada.
- c. He is Jaime Garcia from California.
- d. He is Jason Gatsboukian from Illinois.

40. What did Dan Cody do for Gatsby?
- a. He introduced Gatsby to Daisy on his yacht.
- b. He educated Gatsby about money and the people who have it.
- c. He lent Gatsby money for his early business ventures.
- d. He left Gatsby a fleet of yachts when he died.

41. What is Daisy's opinion of Gatsby's party and how does it affect him?
- a. She likes it immensely. He is so pleased that he asks her to help him arrange his next party.
- b. She doesn't like it. He becomes angry and vows never to see her again.
- c. She doesn't like it. He becomes depressed.
- d. She likes it somewhat. He asks her to attend several more before she gives him her opinion.

42. What does Gatsby want from Daisy?
- a. Gatsby wants her to say she never loved him (Gatsby), so he can be free of her ghost.
- b. He wants to stay friends but not get romantically involved.
- c. He wants her to stay married to Tom and have an affair with him.
- d. He wants her to leave Tom for him to show her unfailing love.

Gatsby Multiple Choice Study Questions Page 9

Chapter 7

43. What was Gatsby's reaction to Daisy's child?
    a. He says he has always dreamed of having children.
    b. He looks at her with surprise.
    c. He backs away, saying that he is uncomfortable around children.
    d. He hugs the child and says she looks just like Daisy.

44. What did Wilson do to Myrtle? Why?
    a. He took her to the hospital to have her broken nose fixed. He wants her to know he loves her and forgives her, no matter what she has done.
    b. He beats her in a jealous rage. He overheard her talking to her sister about Tom.
    c. He locked her in her room. He suspects she is having an affair.
    d. He brought her flowers and promised to be a better husband. He is worried that she will leave him.

45. Why do the four drive into the city on such a hot afternoon?
    a. They have tickets for a Broadway matinee.
    b. Gatsby offers to take them out in the ocean on his yacht.
    c. Nick knows of a hotel that specializes in icy cold baths.
    d. Daisy wants to avoid confrontation and get away from her problems.

46. What does Gatsby think about Daisy's relationship with Tom?
    a. He believes Daisy never loved Tom.
    b. He thinks Daisy will do anything to hurt Tom because he has cheated on her.
    c. He believes that she once loved Tom, but doesn't anymore.
    d. He thinks Daisy loves Tom, but he has never loved her.

47. What is Daisy's reaction to both men?
    a. She realizes that Gatsby is a fraud and decides she is better off with Tom.
    b. She thinks they are both self-centered fools, and she doesn't want either of them.
    c. She wants the escape provided by Gatsby, but needs Tom because he is a lot like her.
    d. She is afraid that Tom will get violent. She thinks she is safer with Gatsby.

48. What happens on the way home from New York?
    a. Nick and Jordan get into an argument and Nick says he will take the train home.
    b. Tom realizes he loves Daisy, and stops at the garage to end his affair with Myrtle
    c. Gatsby is speeding, is stopped by the police and is arrested for drunk driving.
    d. Daisy is driving Gatsby's car. She hits Myrtle Wilson, but keeps driving.

49. Which of these statements about other characters' reactions to Myrtle's death is true?
    a. Wilson thinks he deserved it for cheating on him.
    b. Tom's first instinct is to protect himself. Later he cries.
    c. Nick is not interested because he hardly knows her.
    d. Gatsby thinks he can make up for it by paying Wilson a lot of money.

50. How are Daisy and Tom alike?
    a. They are both arrogant and domineering.
    b. They are both careless, and don't take responsibility for their actions.
    c. They are both consumed with jealousy
    d. They are both unhappy, but too scared to do anything about it.

Gatsby Multiple Choice Study Questions Page 10

Chapter 8

51. What does Gatsby tell Nick about his past?
    a. He knew right away that Daisy only loved him for his money, but she was so lovely and charming that he didn't care.
    b. He was already married when he met Daisy. He was planning to get a divorce after the war so he could marry her.
    c. He knew Daisy was rich, and he wanted to be in control of her fortune.
    d. He fell in love with her and lied about his financial status to impress her.

52. What does Michaelis believe caused Myrtle to run?
    a. She was drunk and didn't know what she was doing.
    b. She saw Tom in the yellow car and was running to him.
    c. She was running away from her husband.
    d. She was trying to make it to the train station on time.

53. Why did she run?
    a. She thought Tom was in the yellow car and was running to him.
    b. Her sister had promised to pick her up and take her to the apartment. She thought the car was her sister's.
    c. She was terrified that Wilson had snapped and was going to kill her.
    d. She thought Tom was through with her, and she tried to commit suicide.

54. Why does Wilson believe that Gatsby killed Myrtle?
    a. An eyewitness identified the car and the driver.
    b. He traces the license number and finds it is Gatsby's.
    c. A mechanic friend gives him the tip.
    d. Tom tells him that the car is Gatsby's.

55. What does Wilson do?
    a. He goes to the police
    b. He kills Gatsby and himself
    c. He leaves the city, a defeated man.
    d. He hires a thug to kill Gatsby and destroy the car.

Gatsby Multiple Choice Study Questions Page 11

Chapter 9

56. Why couldn't Nick get anyone to come to Gatsby's funeral?
    a. The police had roped off the area and no one could get to the house.
    b. Nick didn't have any names and addresses so he could contact people.
    c. In his will, Gatsby had specified that he did not want a crowd at his funeral.
    d. Gatsby had no close friends who really cared about him.

57. Who is Henry C. Gatz?
    a. The undertaker
    b. Gatsby's father
    c. The man who buys Gatsby's house
    d. The owl-eyed man who comes to the funeral

58. Why is the book that Gatsby's father shows Nick important to the novel?
    a. It is a book that Daisy once gave him, and shows that she did love him.
    b. It foreshadows Gatsby's death.
    c. It shows Gatsby's romantic spirit and desire to get ahead.
    d. It is the only memorabilia the father has, and symbolizes his relationship with his son.

59. What happens between Nick and Jordan Baker?
    a. Nick breaks off the relationship because she offends his moral sensibilities.
    b. Nick proposes, but she tells him her golfing career is more important.
    c. Nick leaves new York without contacting her.
    d. Nick tries to break up, but she begs him to stay. He realizes he loves her, and stays with her.

60. What does Nick say about people like Daisy and Tom?
    a. They were dreamers who refused to see reality, but would never really be happy.
    b. They were rich snobs who thought they were above the law and common people.
    c. They were careless people who smashed things and creatures and let others clean up the mess.
    d. They were evil and didn't deserve the wealth they had.

ANSWER KEY - MULTIPLE CHOICE STUDY/QUIZ QUESTIONS
The Great Gatsby

Chapters 1-2

1. B
2. D
3. C
4. A
5. D
6. B
7. A
8. D
9. C
10. A
11. C
12. D
13. A
14. C
15. B
16. D
17. B
18. D
19. C
20. A

Chapter 3

21. C
22. A
23. B
24. D
25. A
26. C
27. B

Chapters 4

28. A
29. D
30. B
31. C
32. D
33. C

Chapter 5 & 6

34. B
35. A
36. B
37. C
38. D
39. A
40. B
41. C
42. D

Chapter 7

43. B
44. C
45. D
46. A
47. C
48. D
49. B
50. B

Chapters 8-9

51. D
52. C
53. A
54. D
55. B
56. D
57. B
58. C
59. A
60. C

PREREADING VOCABULARY WORKSHEETS

VOCABULARY - *The Great Gatsby*

Chapter 1 & 2 Part I: Using Prior Knowledge and Contextual Clues
Below are the sentences in which the vocabulary words above appear in the text. Read the sentence. Use any clues you can find in the sentence combined with your prior knowledge, and write what you think the underlined words mean in the space provided.

1. This isn't just an epigram - life is much more successfully looked at from a single window, after all.

2. Now he was a sturdy, straw haired man of thirty with a rather hard mouth and a supercilious manner.

3. She was only extemporizing but a stirring warmth flowed from her as if her heart was trying to come out to you concealed in one of those breathless, thrilling words.

4. I knew now why her face was familiar-its pleasing contemptuous expression had looked out at me from many rotogravure pictures of the sporting life at . . . Palm Beach.

5. Something was making him nibble at the edge of stale ideas as if his sturdy physical egotism no longer nourished her peremptory heart.

6. Evidently some wild wag of an oculist set them there to fatten his practice . . . and then sank down himself into eternal blindness or forgot them and moved away.

7. The only building in sight was a small block of yellow brick sitting on the edge of the waste land, a sort of compact Main Street ministering to it and contiguous to absolutely nothing.

8. The intense vitality that had been so remarkable in the garage was converted into impressive hauteur.

Part II: Determining the Meaning - Match the vocabulary words to their dictionary definitions.

___ 1. epigram   A. dictatorial; offensively self-assured
___ 2. supercilious   B. adjacent; sharing an edge
___ 3. extemporizing   C. haughtiness in bearing and attitude
___ 4. rotogravure   D. printed material, such as a newspaper
___ 5. peremptory   E. a short, witty poem expressing a single thought
___ 6. oculist   F. feeling or showing haughty disdain
___ 7. contiguous   G. a physician who treats diseases of the eyes
___ 8. hauteur   H. to perform without prior preparation

Vocabulary - *The Great Gatsby* Chapter 3

Part I: Using Prior Knowledge and Contextual Clues
   Below are the sentences in which the vocabulary words above appear in the text. Read the sentence. Use any clues you can find in the sentence combined with your prior knowledge, and write what you think the underlined words mean in the space provided.

1. On week-ends his Rolls-Royce became an omnibus, bearing parties to and from the city, between one in the morning and long past midnight, while his station wagon scampered like a brisk yellow bug to meet all trains.

2. A momentary hush; the orchestra leader varies his rhythm obligingly for her and there is a burst of chatter as the erroneous news goes around what she is Gilda Gray's understudy from the "Follies."

3. There were three married couples and Jordan's escort, a persistent undergraduate given to violent innuendo and obviously under the impression that sooner or later Jordan was going to yield to him her person, to a greater or lesser degree.

4. When the "Jazz History of the World" was over girls were putting their heads on men's shoulders in a puppyish, convivial way, girls were swooning backward playfully into men's arms...

5. Eluding Jordan's undergraduate who was now engaged in an obstetrical conversation with two chorus girls and who implored me to join him, I went inside.

6. The tears coursed down her cheeks-not freely, however, for when they came into contact with her heavily beaded eyelashes they assumed an inky color, and pursued the rest of their way in slow black rivulets.

7. The caterwauling horns had reached a crescendo and I turned away and cut across the lawn toward home.

8. The bored haughty face that she turned to the world concealed something-most affectations conceal something eventually, even though they don't in the beginning-and one day I found what it was.

9. She wasn't able to endure being at a disadvantage, and given this unwillingness I suppose she had begun dealing in subterfuges when she was very young in order to keep that cool insolent smile turned to the world and yet satisfy the demands of her jaunty body.

Vocabulary - *The Great Gatsby* Chapter 3 Continued

Part II: Determining the Meaning   Match the vocabulary words to their dictionary definitions.

___ 1. omnibus
___ 2. erroneous
___ 3. innuendo
___ 4. convivial
___ 5. obstetrical
___ 6. rivulets
___ 7. caterwauling
___ 8. affectations
___ 9. subterfuges

A. medical practice that deals with pregnant women
B. a shrill, discordant sound
C. a show, pretense or display
D. a small brook or stream
E. a long motor vehicle for passengers
F. merry; festive
G. mistaken
H. a deceptive stratagem or device
I. an indirect, derogatory implication in expression

Vocabulary - *The Great Gatsby* Chapters 4 & 5

Part I: Using Prior Knowledge and Contextual Clues
    Below are the sentences in which the vocabulary words above appear in the text. Read the sentence. Use any clues you can find in the sentence combined with your prior knowledge, and write what you think the underlined words mean in the space provided.

1. It was a rich cream color, bright with nickel, swollen here and there in it monstrous length with triumphant hatboxes and supper-boxes and tool-boxes, and terraced with a labyrinth of windshields that mirrored a dozen suns.

2. "After that I lived like a young rajah in all the capitals of Europe-Paris, Venice, Rome- collecting jewels, chiefly rubies, hunting big game, painting a little, things for myself only, and trying to forget something very sad that happened to me long ago.

3. Gatsby took an arm of each of us and moved forward into the restaurant whereupon Mr. Wolfshiem swallowed a new sentence he was starting and lapsed into a somnambulatory abstraction.

4. He's quite a character around New York-a denizen of Broadway."

5. The flowers were unnecessary, for at two o'clock a greenhouse arrived from Gatsby's with innumerable receptacles to contain it.

6. After the house we were to see the grounds and the swimming pool and the hydroplane and the midsummer flowers-but outside Gatsby's window it began to rain again so we stood in a row looking at the corrugated surface of the Sound.

7. He was now decently clothed in a "sport-shirt" open at the neck, sneakers and duck trousers of a nebulous hue.

Vocabulary - *The Great Gatsby* Chapters 4 & 5 Continued

Part II: Determining the Meaning   Match the vocabulary words to their dictionary definitions.

___ 1. labyrinth   A. to walk in a sleep-like condition
___ 2. raja   B. containers that hold items
___ 3. somnambulatory   C. shaped into folds or parallel
___ 4. denizen   D. cloudy, misty, or hazy
___ 5. receptacles   E. prince, or chief in India or East Indies
___ 6. corrugated   F. a intricate structure of interconnecting passages
___ 7. nebulous   G. an inhabitant

Vocabulary - *The Great Gatsby* Chapters 6 & 7

Part I: Using Prior Knowledge and Contextual Clues

Below are the sentences in which the vocabulary words above appear in the text. Read the sentence. Use any clues you can find in the sentence combined with your prior knowledge, and write what you think the underlined words mean in the space provided.

1. He was a son of God - a phrase which, if it means anything, means just that-and he must be about His Father's Business, the service of a vast, vulgar and <u>meretricious</u> beauty.

2. She was appalled by West Egg, this unprecedented "place" that Broadway had begotten upon a Long Island fishing village-appalled by its raw vigor that chafed under the old <u>euphemisms,</u>

3. So the whole <u>caravansary</u> had fallen in like a card house at the disapproval in her eyes.

4. The immediate <u>contingency</u> overtook him, pulled him back from the edge of the theoretical abyss.

5. Her expression was curiously familiar-it was an expression I had often seen on women's faces but on Myrtle Wilson's face it seemed purposeless and <u>inexplicable</u> until I realized that her eyes, wide with jealous terror, were fixed not on Tom but on Jordan Baker, whom she took to be his wife.

6. The transition from <u>libertine</u> to prig was so complete.

7. The circle closed up again with a running murmur of <u>expostulations</u> it was a minute before I could see anything at all.

8. I walked back along the border of the law, <u>traversed</u> the gravel softly and tiptoed up the veranda steps.

9. He put his hands in his coat pockets and turned back eagerly to his <u>scrutiny</u> of the house, as though my presence marred the sacredness of the vigil.

Vocabulary - *The Great Gatsby* Chapters 6 & 7 Continued

Part II: Determining the Meaning   Match the vocabulary words to their dictionary definitions.

___ 1. meretricious
___ 2. euphemisms
___ 3. caravansary
___ 4. contingency
___ 5. inexplicable
___ 6. libertine
___ 7. expostulation
___ 8. traversed
___ 9. scrutiny

A. difficult or impossible to explain or account for
B. close observation
C. attracting attention in a vulgar manner
D. to dissuade or correct
E. a large inn
F. to travel or pass across or over
G. possibility
H. one who acts without moral restraint
I. a vague statement substituted for one considered blunt or offensive

Vocabulary - *The Great Gatsby* Chapters 8 & 9

Part I: Using Prior Knowledge and Contextual Clues
    Below are the sentences in which the vocabulary words above appear in the text. Read the sentence. Use any clues you can find in the sentence combined with your prior knowledge, and write what you think the underlined words mean in the space provided.

1. ... and of romances that were not musty and laid away already in lavender but fresh and breathing and redolent

2. He looked at me anxiously as if he hoped I'd corroborate this.

3. He stopped at the garage for a pneumatic mattress that had amused his guests during the summer, and the chauffeur helped him pump it up.

4. A new world, material without being real, where poor ghosts, breathing dreams like air, drifted fortuitously about...like that ashen, fantastic figure gliding toward him throughout the amorphous trees.

5. ...I thought the whole talk would shortly be served up in racy pasquinade-but Catherine, who might have said anything didn't say a word. [humorous, satirical piece; word not required for test]

6. ...and then hasty addenda beneath:

7. After a little while Mr. Gatz opened the door and came out, his mouth ajar, his face flushed slightly, his eyes leaking isolated and unpunctual tears.

8. The he went into the jewelry store to buy a pearl necklace-or perhaps only a pair of cuff buttons-rid of my provincial squeamishness forever.

9. I went over and looked at that huge incoherent failure of a house once more.

Vocabulary - *The Great Gatsby* Chapters 8 & 9 Continued

10. Its vanished trees, the trees that had made way for Gatsby's house, had once <u>pandered</u> in whispers to the last and greatest of all human dreams;

11. ...face to face for the last time in history with something <u>commensurate</u> to his capacity for wonder.

Part II: Determining the Meaning   Match the vocabulary words to their dictionary definitions.

___ 1. redolent   A. something added, especially a supplement to a book
___ 2. corroborate   B. to act as a go-between in sexual intrigues
___ 3. pneumatic   C. limited in perspective
___ 4. amorphous   D. unable to think in a clear or orderly manner
___ 5. addenda   E. corresponding in size or degree
___ 6 unpunctual   F. to strengthen or support with other evidence
___ 7. provincial   G. relating to air or other gases
___ 8. incoherent   H. lacking definite form
___ 9. pandered   I. late
___ 10. commensurate   J. suggestive

ANSWER KEY - VOCABULARY
The Great Gatsby

Chapters 1 & 2
1. E
2. F
3. H
4. D
5. A
6. G
7. B
8. C

Chapter 3
1. E
2. G
3. I
4. F
5. A
6. D
7. B
8. C
9. H

Chapters 4 & 5
1. F
2. E
3. A
4. G
5. B
6. C
7. D

Chapters 6 & 7
1. C
2. I
3. E
4. G
5. A
6. H
7. D
8. F
9. B

Chapters 8 & 9
1. J
2. F
3. G
4. H
5. A
6. I
7. C
8. D
9. B
10. E

DAILY LESSONS

LESSON ONE

Objectives
1. To introduce the *Great Gatsby* unit.
2. To distribute books and other related materials
3. To preview the study questions for chapters 1-2
4. To familiarize students with the vocabulary for chapters 1-2

Activity #1

Explain to students that you will be reading *The Great Gatsby* by F. Scott Fitzgerald and that the novel takes place in the Roaring Twenties. Ask students what they know about the "Roaring Twenties."

Show a film or video with background information about the 1920's in America. If a film is not available, invite a guest speaker from a local museum or historical society (or perhaps you know someone who lived through the 1920's who could come and talk and answer questions. Another option is to offer some extra-credit work for students who will research and make an oral report about the 1920's and F. Scott Fitzgerald.

Activity #2

Distribute the materials students will use in this unit. Explain in detail how students are to use these materials.

Study Guides Students should read the study guide questions for each reading assignment prior to beginning the reading assignment to get a feeling for what events and ideas are important in the section they are about to read. After reading the section, students will (as a class or individually) answer the questions to review the important events and ideas from that section of the book. Students should keep the study guides as study materials for the unit test.

Vocabulary Prior to reading a reading assignment, students will do vocabulary work related to the section of the book they are about to read. Following the completion of the reading of the book, there will be a vocabulary review of all the words used in the vocabulary assignments. Students should keep their vocabulary work as study materials for the unit test.

Reading Assignment Sheet You need to fill in the reading assignment sheet to let students know by when their reading has to be completed. You can either write the assignment sheet up on a side blackboard or bulletin board and leave it there for students to see each day, or you can "ditto" copies for each student to have. In either case, you should advise students to become very familiar with the reading assignments so they know what is expected of them.

<u>Extra Activities Center</u> The resource materials portion of this unit contains suggestions for an extra library of related books and articles in your classroom as well as crossword and word search puzzles. Make an extra activities center in your room where you will keep these materials for students to use. (Bring the books and articles in from the library and keep several copies of the puzzles on hand.) Explain to students that these materials are available for students to use when they finish reading assignments or other class work early.

<u>Nonfiction Assignment Sheet</u> Explain to students that they each are to read at least one non-fiction piece from the in-class library at some time during the unit. Students will fill out a nonfiction assignment sheet after completing the reading to help you evaluate their reading experiences and to help the students think about and evaluate their own reading experiences.

<u>Books</u> Each school has its own rules and regulations regarding student use of school books. Advise students of the procedures that are normal for your school.

Activity #3

Preview the study questions and have students do the vocabulary work for Chapters 1-2 of *The Great Gatsby*. If students do not finish this assignment during this class period, they should complete it prior to the next class meeting.

NONFICTION ASSIGNMENT SHEET
(To be completed after reading the required nonfiction article)

Name _____ Date _____

Title of Nonfiction Read _____

Written By _____ Publication Date _____

I. Factual Summary: Write a short summary of the piece you read.

II. Vocabulary
    1. With which vocabulary words in the piece did you encounter some degree of difficulty?

    2. How did you resolve your lack of understanding with these words?

III. Interpretation: What was the main point the author wanted you to get from reading his work?

IV. Criticism
    1. With which points of the piece did you agree or find easy to accept? Why?

    2. With which points of the piece did you disagree or find difficult to believe? Why?

V. Personal Response: What do you think about this piece? OR How does this piece influence your ideas?

LESSON TWO

Objectives
1. To read chapters 1-2
2. To give students practice reading orally
3. To evaluate students' oral reading

Activity

Have students read chapters 1-2 of *The Great Gatsby* out loud in class. You probably know the best way to get readers with your class; pick students at random, ask for volunteers, or use whatever method works best for your group. If you have not yet completed an oral reading evaluation for your students this marking period, this would be a good opportunity to do so. A form is included with this unit for your convenience.

If students do not complete reading chapters 1-2 in class, they should do so prior to your next class meeting.

LESSON THREE

Objectives
1. To review the main events and ideas from chapters 1-2
2. To preview the study questions for chapter 3
3. To familiarize students with the vocabulary in chapter 3
4. To read chapter 3

Activity #1

Give students a few minutes to formulate answers for the study guide questions for chapters 1-2, and then discuss the answers to the questions in detail. Write the answers on the board or overhead transparency so students can have the correct answers for study purposes. Note: It is a good practice in public speaking and leadership skills for individual students to take charge of leading the discussions of the study questions. Perhaps a different student could go to the front of the class and lead the discussion each day that the study questions are discussed during this unit. Of course, the teacher should guide the discussion when appropriate and be sure to fill in any gaps the students leave.

Activity #2

Give students about fifteen minutes to preview the study questions for chapter 3 of *The Great Gatsby* and to do the related vocabulary work.

Activity #3

Assign students to read chapter 3 of *The Great Gatsby* prior to your next class period. If there is time remaining in this period, students may begin reading silently.

ORAL READING EVALUATION - *The Great Gatsby*

Name _____ Class____ Date _____

SKILL	EXCELLENT	GOOD	AVERAGE	FAIR	POOR
Fluency	5	4	3	2	1
Clarity	5	4	3	2	1
Audibility	5	4	3	2	1
Pronunciation	5	4	3	2	1
_____	5	4	3	2	1
_____	5	4	3	2	1

Total _____ Grade _____

Comments:

LESSON FOUR

Objectives
1. To check to see that students read chapter 3 as assigned
2. To review the main ideas and events from chapter 3
3. To preview the study questions for chapters 4-5
4. To familiarize students with the vocabulary in chapters 4-5
5. To read chapters 4-5
6. To evaluate students' oral reading

Activity #1
Quiz - Distribute quizzes and give students about 10 minutes to complete them. (Note: The quizzes may either be the short answer study guides or the multiple choice version.) Have students exchange papers. Grade the quizzes as a class. Collect the papers for recording the grades. (If you used the multiple choice version as a quiz, take a few minutes to discuss the answers for the short answer version if your students are using the short answer version for their study guides.)

Activity #2
Give students about 15 minutes to preview the study questions for chapters 4-5 and to do the related vocabulary work.

Activity #3
Have students read chapters 4-5 orally for the remainder of the class period. Continue the oral reading evaluations. If students do not complete reading these chapters during this class period, they should do so prior to your next class meeting.

LESSON FIVE

Objectives
1. To review the main ideas and events from chapters 4-5
2. To give students the opportunity to practice writing to inform
3. To have students look more closely at the characters in the novel
4. To show students that details in the story help to support and form the characters
5. To give the teacher the opportunity to evaluate students' writing skills

Activity #1
Give students a few minutes to formulate answers to the study guide questions for chapters 4-5. Discuss the answers to the questions in detail.

Activity #2
Distribute Writing Assignment #1 and discuss the directions in detail. Allow the remaining class time for students to complete the assignment. Collect the papers at the end of the class period.

Follow - Up: After you have graded the assignments, have a writing conference with the students. (This unit schedules one in Lesson Seven.) After the writing conference, allow students to revise their papers using your suggestions and corrections. Give them about three days from the date they receive their papers to complete the revision. I suggest grading the revisions on an A-C-E scale (all revisions well-done, some revisions made, few or no revisions made). This will speed your grading time and still give some credit for the students' efforts.

WRITING ASSIGNMENT #1 - *The Great Gatsby*

PROMPT
We have briefly discussed the homes of Nick, the Buchanans and Gatsby. Your assignment is to describe each of their homes and explain how the home of each corresponds to the social position, lifestyle and personality of the owners.

PREWRITING
One way to begin is to jot down notes describing each house. Go back and decide what social position each owner holds and which personal characteristics are relevant. Then jot down notes as to how each home suits the owner.

DRAFTING
Write an opening (introductory) paragraph in which you introduce the idea that each of the homes suits the characteristics of its owners.

In the body of your composition, write one paragraph about each home/owner combination. In each of these body paragraphs, start with a sentence which will let your reader know about which home/owner combination the paragraph is about (a topic sentence). Follow that with the information you have about the home/owner combination.

Write a concluding paragraph in which you summarize your ideas and make your final statements and conclusions.

PROMPT
When you finish the rough draft of your paper, ask a student who sits near you to read it. After reading your rough draft, he/she should tell you what he/she liked best about your work, which parts were difficult to understand, and ways in which your work could be improved. Reread your paper considering your critic's comments, and make the corrections you think are necessary.

PROOFREADING
Do a final proofreading of your paper double-checking your grammar, spelling, organization, and the clarity of your ideas.

LESSON SIX

Objectives
1. To preview the study questions and vocabulary for chapters 6 & 7
2. To read chapters 6 & 7

Activity #1
Give students about ten minutes to complete the prereading work for chapters 6 & 7.

Activity #2
Have students read chapters 6 & 7 orally in class. If you have not yet completed the oral reading evaluations, this would be a good time to do so. If students do not complete reading chapters 6 & 7 orally in class, they should read them independently prior to the next class period.

LESSON SEVEN

Objectives
1. To review the main events of chapters 6 & 7
2. To assign the pre-reading, vocabulary and reading work for chapters 8-9
3. To give the teacher time to talk with students about their writing skills

Activity #1
Give students a few minutes to formulate answers to the study guide questions for chapters 6 & 7. Discuss the answers to the questions in detail.

Activity #2
Give students about ten minutes to do the prereading work for chapters 8-9.

Activity #3
Tell students that prior to the next period they should have completed reading *The Great Gatsby*. Give students this class period to read chapters 8-9 silently to complete reading the book. If students do not finish this assignment in class, they should do so prior to the next class meeting.

Activity #4
While students are reading, call students to your desk (or some other private area) to discuss their papers from Writing Assignment 1. A Writing Evaluation Form is included with this unit to help structure your conferences.

WRITING EVALUATION FORM - *The Great Gatsby*

Name _____ Date _____

Writing Assignment #1 for the *Great Gatsby* unit   Grade _____

Circle One For Each Item:

Grammar:	correct	errors noted on paper
Spelling:	correct	errors noted on paper
Punctuation:	correct	errors noted on paper
Legibility:	excellent	good fair poor
_____	excellent	good fair poor
_____	excellent	good fair poor

Strengths:

Weaknesses:

Comments/Suggestions:

LESSON EIGHT

Objectives
1. To review the main ideas of chapters 8-9
2. To discuss the development of the main characters in *The Great Gatsby*

Activity #1
Give students a few minutes to formulate answers to the study questions for chapters 8-9. Discuss the answers to the questions in detail.

Activity #2
Divide your class into ten groups. Assign each of the groups one of the following characters: Gatsby, Nick, Tom, Daisy, Jordan, George Wilson, Myrtle Wilson, Mr. Wolfshiem, Pammy and Owl Eyes.

Each group should be prepared to give the following information: a physical description, a description of the character's personality (with examples for support), any evidence of growth or change in the person throughout the novel, social standing, purpose in the novel, and any indications as to whether the character is a "good guy" or a "bad guy."

Give students ample time to prepare the required information.

Activity #3
Take class time to discuss each of the characters the groups have been assigned. A large chart on the board or overhead projector would make a good aid. Place the characters' names in the left-hand column, and then in each of six columns to the right, place information about the six points mentioned in activity #2.

LESSON NINE

Objectives
1. To give students the opportunity to practice writing to persuade
2. To expand and evaluate students' understanding of the characters in the book
3. To give the teacher the opportunity to evaluate students' writing skills

Activity
Distribute Writing Assignment #2. Discuss the directions in detail and give students ample time to complete the assignment.

WRITING ASSIGNMENT #2 - *The Great Gatsby*

PROMPT

Now that you have completed reading *The Great Gatsby* and have spent some time talking about the characters, you should pretty well understand the characters, their attitudes, and the things that motivate them.

Your assignment is to write one of the following letters:
1. from Gatsby to Daisy persuading her to leave Tom for him
2. from Nick to Gatsby persuading him to give up his hopes for a relationship with Daisy
3. from Jordan to Nick persuading him to pursue his relationship with her
4. from Myrtle to Tom persuading him to leave Daisy for her

PREWRITING

Choose which of the letters you think you would like to write. Think about the character who is doing the writing (the character you must pretend to be as you write the letter). Now think about the person to whom you are writing. Jot down a list of three or four things that would be most likely to persuade that person to do what you want him/her to do.

Which of those things would make your best argument (would be most likely to persuade the person)? Put a star next to that one. Number the remaining items on your list from most persuasive to least persuasive.

DRAFTING

Begin your composition in a letter format. Use the introductory paragraph to introduce the idea you wish to convey in your letter.

In the body of your letter, write one paragraph for each of your persuasive arguments. Some people prefer to write from the least persuasive to the most persuasive arguments. Others prefer to begin with the most persuasive argument and then work from the least persuasive to the second most persuasive arguments. How do you decide which to do? Consider your arguments and your audience. What do you think will work best in your particular situation? After careful consideration, write your paper with the organization you think best suits your situation.

Your closing paragraph could be done in a number of ways. You might give your final thoughts or make a final pitch or plea. You could end either firmly or with a more mellow tone. If your entire letter has been firm, consider whether you should keep that tone or write a few lines in a more mellow tone. The way you will close your letter will depend entirely on you and the impression with which you want to leave your reader.

PROMPT

When you finish the rough draft of your paper, ask a student who sits near you to read it. After reading your rough draft, he/she should tell you what he/she liked best about your work, which parts were difficult to understand, and ways in which your work could be improved. Reread your paper considering your critic's comments, and make the corrections you think are necessary, and then do a final proofreading of your work.

LESSON TEN

Objective
To review all of the vocabulary work done in this unit

Activity
Choose one (or more) of the vocabulary review activities listed below and spend your class period as directed in the activity. Some of the materials for these review activities are located in the Vocabulary Resource section of this unit.

VOCABULARY REVIEW ACTIVITIES

1. Divide your class into two teams and have an old-fashioned spelling or definition bee.

2. Give each of your students (or students in groups of two, three or four) a *The Great Gatsby* Vocabulary Word Search Puzzle. The person (group) to find all of the vocabulary words in the puzzle first wins.

3. Give students a *The Great Gatsby* Vocabulary Word Search Puzzle without the word list. The person or group to find the most vocabulary words in the puzzle wins.

4. Use a *The Great Gatsby* Vocabulary Crossword Puzzle. Put the puzzle onto a transparency on the overhead projector (so everyone can see it), and do the puzzle together as a class.

5. Give students a *The Great Gatsby* Vocabulary Matching Worksheet to do.

6. Divide your class into two teams. Use the *Great Gatsby* vocabulary words with their letters jumbled as a word list. Student 1 from Team A faces off against Student 1 from Team B. You write the first jumbled word on the board. The first student (1A or 1B) to unscramble the word wins the chance for his/her team to score points. If 1A wins the jumble, go to student 2A and give him/her a definition. He/she must give you the correct spelling of the vocabulary word which fits that definition. If he/she does, Team A scores a point, and you give student 3A a definition for which you expect a correctly spelled matching vocabulary word. Continue giving Team A definitions until some team member makes an incorrect response. An incorrect response sends the game back to the jumbled-word face off, this time with students 2A and 2B. Instead of repeating giving definitions to the first few students of each team, continue with the student after the one who gave the last incorrect response on the team. For example, if Team B wins the jumbled-word face-off, and student 5B gave the last incorrect answer for Team B, you would start this round of definition questions with student 6B, and so on. The team with the most points wins!

8. Have students write a story in which they correctly use as many vocabulary words as possible. Have students read their compositions orally! Post the most original compositions on your bulletin board!

LESSON ELEVEN

Objectives
    1. To study the conflicts, symbols and images in *The Great Gatsby*
    2. To give students the opportunity to practice working together in small groups
    3. To help students review the text and find important ideas they may have missed on the first reading
    4. To give students the opportunity to practice their public speaking skills
    5. To gather basic information which will be used later in a discussion of the themes of the novel

Activity #1

    Divide your class into 9 groups -- one group for each chapter (or 5 groups, one for each reading assignment). Allow the groups time to find the conflicts and anything they think may be a symbol or image important to the novel in their chapters. Allow time for the group members to discuss their findings and come up with some intelligent statements about their findings. The groups should appoint one spokesperson to report the group's findings regarding conflicts, another spokesperson to identify the symbols and images, and a third spokesperson to give the group's thoughts regarding their findings.

Activity #2

    Call on individual group members by chapter(s) to give their information. Jot them down briefly for students to copy into their notes. Allow time for discussion and questions about each point.
    Ask if anyone from the group has anything to add.

NOTE: If group reports don't finish during this class period, finish them at the beginning of Lesson 9.

LESSON TWELVE

Objectives
1. To complete the small group reports about conflict, symbols and images.
2. To continue the discussion of *The Great Gatsby* and enlarge it to put together all of the information collected in the last several lessons into some statements of the themes of the novel
3. To direct students' attention to some points which may have been overlooked in previous discussions

Activity #1
Complete the reports from Lesson Eleven.

Activity #2
Introduce the formula:
CHARACTER + PLOT + CONFLICT + SYMBOLS + IMAGES + NARRATIVE TECHNIQUE = THEME

Tell students that over the past several days, they have been gathering information about each of the parts of this formula, and that today you are going to put the parts together.

You have discussed character, conflict, symbols and images through large and small group work. The plot has been discussed in the study guides as well as indirectly in the other discussions. Now, you need to take a look at narrative technique for a few minutes. This should include information about Nick as the narrator (advantages and use), the method of revealing mysterious Gatsby's character, and the use of dialogue at critical events to heighten the drama (instead of everything being told as "Nick said").

You may want to include a few miscellaneous points about the seasons (spring when Nick comes, summer when action gets "hot" and fall when Nick leaves) and the songs (reflect the ideas of the age and Gatsby's characters).

At this point, ask students to come up with some ideas as to the point of the novel; the main idea(s) Fitzgerald was trying to get across to his readers through the use of his literary tools. Allow time for discussion.

Activity #3
Take a few minutes to discuss the Extra Discussion Questions/Writing Assignments you think are appropriate for your class.

EXTRA WRITING ASSIGNMENTS/DISCUSSION QUESTIONS - *The Great Gatsby*

Interpretation

1. From what point of view is *The Great Gatsby* written, and what effect does that have on the story?

2. Is the story of *The Great Gatsby* believable? Explain why or why not.

3. Where is the climax of the story? Explain your choice.

4. Are the characters in *The Great Gatsby* stereotypes? If so, explain the usefulness of employing stereotypes in the novel. If they are not, explain how they merit individuality.

5. What is the setting of the story? Could this story have been set in a different time and place and still have the same effect?

Critical

6. Describe Gatsby's relationship with Daisy.

7. Are Gatsby's actions believably motivated? Explain why or why not.

8. Evaluate F. Scott Fitzgerald's style of writing. How does it contribute to the value of the novel?

9. Compare and contrast Gatsby and Tom.

10. Compare and contrast Daisy and Myrtle.

11. Explain how F. Scott Fitzgerald uses the minor characters--Owl Eyes, Mr. Wolfshiem, Pammy, Michaelis, and George Wilson in the novel. What does each character add to the story?

12. Explain how the title, *The Great Gatsby*, is appropriate.

13. What is Nick's role in *Gatsby*? What does he add to the story, and how would the story have been different without him?

14. Who was responsible for Gatsby's death? Explain your choice.

15. Why did Fitzgerald "kill off" Gatsby? What did this plot choice add to the story?

The Great Gatsby Extra Discussion Questions page 2

16. What was the importance of Myrtle's death? How would the story have changed if Myrtle had <u>not</u> been killed?

17. How was Nick different from Daisy, Tom and Jordan?

18. Was Gatsby different from Daisy, Tom and Jordan? Explain your answer.

19. Why do Daisy and Tom stay together?

<u>Personal Response</u>

20. Did you enjoy reading *The Great Gatsby*? Why or why not?

21. Would you have liked to have been a part of Gatsby's social circle? Explain why or why not.

22. What does it mean to be rich? Do responsibilities come with money? Did Gatsby's money bring him happiness?

23. Suppose this novel had been written from Gatsby's point of view. How would the story have changed?

24. What would you do if you had as much money as Gatsby?

LESSON THIRTEEN

Objective
> To look at some passages from the novel and discuss their meaning and importance to the theme(s).

Activity #1
> Now that you have discussed some themes from the novel, there are several passages which are worthwhile to review in relationship to the themes.
>
> A page of quotations follows. Distribute a copy of the quotes to each student. You could either discuss the quotes orally or have the students work independently to jot down the significance of each quote and then have an oral discussion. I believe the latter method usually works best.

Activity #2
> If time remains in the period, give students a chance to review and get their notes in order for the review lesson which follows.

QUOTATIONS - *The Great Gatsby*

1. "Gatsby turned out all right in the end." (Nick)

2. "You live in West Egg," she remarked contemptuously. (Jordan to Nick)

3. "I hate that word hulking," objected Tom crossly, "even in kidding." . . . "Hulking," insisted Daisy.

4. "I suppose she talks and -- eats, and everything." (Daisy about Pammy)

5. ". . . after that they conducted themselves according to the rules of behavior associated with an amusement park." (Nick about Gatsby's party guests)

6. "Sometimes they came and went without having met Gatsby at all, came for the party with a simplicity of heart that was its own ticket of admission." (Nick about Gatsby's party guests)

7. "The books? . . . Absolutely real -- have pages and everything. I thought they'd be made of cardboard." (Owl Eyes to Nick and Jordan in Gatsby's library)

8. "He's just a man named Gatsby."

9. "I wondered if the fact that he was not drinking helped to set him off from his guests." (Nick about Gatsby)

10. "He came alive to me, delivered suddenly from the womb of his purposeless splendor." (Nick about Gatsby when he realized Gatsby's dream)

11. ". . . he stared around at his possessions in a dazed way, as though in her actual astounding presence none of it was any longer real." (Nick about Gatsby when he showed him his house)

Gatsby Quotations Page 2

12. "He had been full of the idea so long . . . Now in the reaction, he was running down like an over-wound clock." (Nick about Gatsby after he had met with Daisy)

13. "Possibly it had occurred to him that the colossal significance of the [green] light had now vanished forever." (Nick about Gatsby after he had met with Daisy)

14. "There must have been moments even that afternoon when Daisy tumbled short of his dreams
    -- not through her own fault, but because of the colossal vitality of his illusion. It had gone beyond her, beyond everything." (Nick about Gatsby after he had met with Daisy)

15. "I wouldn't ask too much of her," I ventured. "You can't repeat the past." (Nick to Gatsby about Daisy)

16. "He knew that when he kissed this girl, and forever wed his unutterable visions to her perishable breath, his mind would not romp again like the mind of God." (Nick of Gatsby)

17. "So the whole caravansary had fallen in like a card house at the disapproval of her eyes." (Nick after Daisy had come to Gatsby's party)

18. "What'll we do with ourselves this afternoon?" cried Daisy, "and the day after that, and the next thirty years?"

19. "But it's so hot," insisted Daisy, . . ." and everything is so confused. Let's all go to town."

20. "Ah," she cried, "you look so cool." (Daisy to Gatsby in front of Tom)

21. "You resemble the advertisement of the man," she went on innocently. (Daisy to Gatsby in front of Tom)

Gatsby Quotations Page 3

22. "Her voice is full of money." (Gatsby to Nick about Daisy)

23. ". . . and it occurred to me that there was no difference between men, in intelligence or race, so profound as the difference between the sick and the well. Wilson was so sick that he looked guilty. . . ." (Nick after the accident)

24. "Nowadays people begin by sneering at family life and family institutions, and next they'll throw everything overboard and have intermarriage between black and white." (Tom after he finds out about Daisy's affair)

25. "I was thirty." (Nick)

26. ". . . anybody would have said that they were conspiring together." (Nick as he looked at Tom and Daisy in their home after the accident)

27. "So I walked away and left him standing there in the moonlight -- watching over nothing." (Nick about Gatsby's remaining outside Daisy's house after the accident)

28. "They're a rotten crowd," I shouted across the lawn. "You're worth the whole damn bunch put together." (Nick to Gatsby)

29. "They were careless people, Tom and Daisy." (Nick)

30. "So we beat on, boats against the current, borne back ceaselessly into the past."

LESSONS FOURTEEN AND FIFTEEN

Objectives
1. To tie together the "fact" and "fiction" elements of the story
2. To give students some practical application related to *Gatsby*
3. To show students how to plan an elegant party rather than the "keg and pizza" type which are more common today
4. To let students have some fun while learning about the 1920's

Activity #1

Take your class to the library. Explain to your class that they are going to recreate one of Gatsby's parties. To do so properly, this activity will be divided into three stages: research, planning, and actually having the party.

Divide your class into five groups, one "committee" for each of the following: invitations, food, entertainment, decorations and etiquette. Tell students that for the research stage, each group is responsible for finding out how its topic would have been done in the 1920's. How did one make a guest list and write out the invitations? What kinds of food were most popular at parties? What kinds of entertainment would have been appropriate? How would the setting of the party have looked? How would the guests been expected to behave? These are the kinds of things students should find the answers to in this class period.

Activity #2

After students have done their research, they should move to stage two of this assignment: planning.

Now that they know what kinds of things were done, they now are to plan how they will recreate these things for their own "Gatsby Party." The invitation committee should actually make invitations to the party. The food committee should actually plan what food will be served, who will make it, and how it will be served. The entertainment committee should decide upon the appropriate entertainment and find a way to recreate that at the party. The etiquette committee needs to let everyone know how they are to act at the party, how the table is to be set, etc. The decorations committee should plan ways to make the setting of the party appropriate.

Notes: Each student should be assigned a role to play on the day of the party. You will need Gatsby and all the major characters of the book as well as people to serve the food, perhaps provide entertainment, etc. Be sure to assign a role to each student.

Students should dress the part of their character on the day of the party.

Be sure to tell students that the party is scheduled for Lesson Eighteen. (Give students a day and a date so there will be no confusion.)

LESSON SIXTEEN

Objectives
1. To widen the breadth of students' knowledge about the topics discussed or touched upon in *The Great Gatsby*
2. To check students' nonfiction reading assignments

Activity

Ask each student to give a brief oral report about the nonfiction work he/she read for the nonfiction reading assignment. Your criteria for evaluating this report will vary depending on the level of your students. You may wish for students to give a complete report without using notes of any kind, or you may want students to read directly from a written report, or you may want to do something in between these two extremes. Just make students aware of your criteria in ample time for them to prepare their reports.

Start with one student's report. After that, ask if anyone else in the class has read on a topic related to the first student's report. If no one has, choose another student at random. After each report, be sure to ask if anyone has a report related to the one just completed. That will help keep a continuity during the discussion of the reports.

LESSON SEVENTEEN

Objectives
    1. To give students the opportunity to express their own opinions
    2. To exercise students' imaginations
    3. To give the teacher the opportunity to evaluate students' writing

Activity
    Distribute Writing Assignment #3 and discuss the directions in detail. Give students the entire class period to work on this assignment, and then collect the papers for grading.

LESSON EIGHTEEN

Objectives
    1. To tie together the "fact" and "fiction" elements of the story
    2. To give students some practical application related to *Gatsby*
    3. To show students how to plan an elegant party rather than the "keg and pizza" type which are more common today
    4. To let students have some fun while learning about the 1920's
    5. To actually have a Gatsby Party for which the students have planned

Activity
    Give students the entire class period to perform their Gatsby Party.

LESSON NINETEEN

Objective
    To review the main ideas presented in *The Great Gatsby*

Activity #1
    Choose one of the review games/activities included in the packet and spend your class period as outlined there. Some materials for these activities are located in the Extra Activities Packet section of this unit.

Activity #2
    Remind students that the Unit Test will be in the next class meeting. Stress the review of the Study Guides and their class notes as a last minute, brush-up review for homework.

WRITING ASSIGNMENT #3 - *The Great Gatsby*

PROMPT
"Jimmy was bound to get ahead. He always had some resolves like this or something." Gatsby's became wealthy and educated wasn't an accident. He had to work for it. He set goals for himself, learned things, and worked towards his goals.

Your assignment is to write a composition in which you outline the things you hope to do with your life and the ways in which you can work towards fulfilling those ideals.

PREWRITING
One way to start is to jot down the things you want from your future. Which things are most important to you? Next to each item write down things you can do to help yourself achieve that goal.

DRAFTING
Begin with an introductory paragraph telling what you would like your future to be. In the body of your paper, write one paragraph for each of your goals. Within each paragraph write ways in which you can help yourself achieve each goal. Finally, write a concluding paragraph in which you give a little analysis of whether you think you will actually be able to do the things you have set forth for yourself to do.

PROMPT
When you finish the rough draft of your paper, ask a student who sits near you to read it. After reading your rough draft, he/she should tell you what he/she liked best about your work, which parts were difficult to understand, and ways in which your work could be improved. Reread your paper considering your critic's comments, and make the corrections you think are necessary.

PROOFREADING
Do a final proofreading of your paper double-checking your grammar, spelling, organization, and the clarity of your ideas.

REVIEW GAMES/ACTIVITIES - *The Great Gatsby*

1. Ask the class to make up a unit test for *The Great Gatsby*. The test should have 4 sections: matching, true/false, short answer, and essay. Students may use 1/2 period to make the test and then swap papers and use the other 1/2 class period to take a test a classmate has devised. (open book) You may want to use the unit test included in this packet or take questions from the students' unit tests to formulate your own test.

2. Take 1/2 period for students to make up true and false questions (including the answers). Collect the papers and divide the class into two teams. Draw a big tic-tac-toe board on the chalk board. Make one team X and one team O. Ask questions to each side, giving each student one turn. If the question is answered correctly, that students' team's letter (X or O) is placed in the box. If the answer is incorrect, no mark is placed in the box. The object is to get three marks in a row like tic-tac-toe. You may want to keep track of the number of games won for each team.

3. Take 1/2 period for students to make up questions (true/false and short answer). Collect the questions. Divide the class into two teams. You'll alternate asking questions to individual members of teams A & B (like in a spelling bee). The question keeps going from A to B until it is correctly answered, then a new question is asked. A correct answer does not allow the team to get another question. Correct answers are +2 points; incorrect answers are -1 point.

4. Have students pair up and quiz each other from their study guides and class notes.

5. Give students a *The Great Gatsby* crossword puzzle to complete.

6. Divide your class into two teams. Use the *Great Gatsby* crossword words with their letters jumbled as a word list. Student 1 from Team A faces off against Student 1 from Team B. You write the first jumbled word on the board. The first student (1A or 1B) to unscramble the word wins the chance for his/her team to score points. If 1A wins the jumble, go to student 2A and give him/her a clue. He/she must give you the correct word which matches that clue. If he/she does, Team A scores a point, and you give student 3A a clue for which you expect another correct response. Continue giving Team A clues until some team member makes an incorrect response. An incorrect response sends the game back to the jumbled-word face off, this time with students 2A and 2B. Instead of repeating giving clues to the first few students of each team, continue with the student after the one who gave the last incorrect response on the team. For example, if Team B wins the jumbled-word face-off, and student 5B gave the last incorrect answer for Team B, you would start this round of clue questions with student 6B, and so on. The team with the most points wins!

UNIT TESTS

SHORT ANSWER UNIT TEST 1 - *The Great Gatsby*

I. Matching/Identify

___ 1. Gatsby   A. The Great Gatsby

___ 2. Nick   B. Daisy's little girl

___ 3. Tom   C. Nick has a short affair with her

___ 4. Daisy   D. Showed Gatsby how to live in the rich man's world

___ 5. Jordan   E. The woman with whom Gatsby wants a relationship

___ 6. Myrtle   F. Narrator; Gatsby's neighbor

___ 7. George   G. His car ran over Myrtle

___ 8. Wolfshiem   H. Gatsby's father

___ 9. Klipspringer   I. Business associate of Gatsby

___ 10. Owl Eyes   J. Tom has an affair with her

___ 11. Henry Gatz   K. Nick & Jordan meet him in Gatsby's library

___ 12. James Gatz   L. Daisy's husband

___ 13. Pammy   M. "The Boarder"

___ 14. Cody   N. Myrtle's husband

II. Short Answer

1. How is Gatsby introduced into the novel?

2. What did Tom do to Myrtle when she mentioned Daisy's name?

Gatsby Short Answer Unit Test 1 Page 2

3. Describe Gatsby's wealth. List some of the things that represent wealth.

4. What kind of people come to Gatsby's parties?

5. What does Jordan tell Nick about Daisy, Gatsby and Tom?

6. Why did Gatsby want Daisy to see the house and his clothes?

7. What had the green light on the dock meant to Gatsby?

8. Why do the four drive into the city on such a hot afternoon?

9. What happens on the way home from New York?

10. Why does Wilson believe that Gatsby killed Myrtle?

11. What does Wilson do?

12. What does Nick say about people like Daisy and Tom?

Gatsby Short Answer Unit Test 1 Page 3

III. Composition

What is the point of *The Great Gatsby*? When we read books, we usually come away from our reading experience a little richer, having given more thought to a particular aspect of life. What do you think F. Scott Fitzgerald intended us to gain from reading his novel?

Gatsby Short Answer Unit Test 1 Page 4

IV. Vocabulary
    Listen to the vocabulary words and write them down.
    Go back later and fill in the correct definition for each word.

1.

2.

3.

4.

5.

6.

7.

8.

9.

10.

SHORT ANSWER UNIT TEST 2 - *The Great Gatsby*

I. Matching

___ 1. Gatsby   A. Myrtle's husband

___ 2. Nick   B. "The Boarder"

___ 3. Tom   C. Daisy's husband

___ 4. Daisy   D. Nick and Jordan met him in Gatsby's library

___ 5. Jordan   E. Tom had an affair with her

___ 6. Myrtle   F. Business associate of Gatsby

___ 7. George   G. Gatsby's father

___ 8. Wolfshiem   H. Extremely wealthy man who throws extravagant parties

___ 9. Klipspringer   I. Narrator; Gatsby's neighbor

___ 10. Owl Eyes   J. The woman with whom Gatsby wants to resume a relationship

___ 11. Henry Gatz   K. Showed Gatsby how to live in the rich man's world

___ 12. James Gatz   L. Nick had a short affair with her

___ 13. Pammy   M. Daisy's little girl

___ 14. Cody   N. The Great Gatsby

II. Short Answer

1. When asked about her daughter, what does Daisy say?

2. What are the "eyes of Dr. T. J. Eckleburg?

3. What does Jordan tell Nick about Daisy, Gatsby and Tom?

Gatsby Short Answer Unit Test 2 Page 2

4. What had Gatsby turned Daisy into in his own mind?

5. What is Daisy's opinion of Gatsby's party? How does this affect him?

4. What does Gatsby want from Daisy?

5. What happens on the way home from New York?

6. How do these people react to Myrtle's death:
   a. Wilson:

   b. Tom:

   c. Gatsby:

7. What is the book Henry Gatz shows Nick? Why is it important to the novel?

8. What does Nick say about people like Daisy and Tom?

Gatsby Short Answer Unit Test 2 Page 3

III. Composition

    F. Scott Fitzgerald wrote *The Great Gatsby* in 1925, and here we are reading it so many years later. Why? What makes this book a "classic"?

Gatsby Short Answer Unit Test 1 Page 4

IV. Vocabulary
   Listen to the vocabulary words and write them down.
   Go back later and fill in the correct definition for each word.

1.

2.

3.

4.

5.

6.

7.

8.

9.

10.

KEY: SHORT ANSWER UNIT TESTS - *The Great Gatsby*

The short answer questions are taken directly from the study guides.
If you need to look up the answers, you will find them in the study guide section.

Answers to the composition questions will vary depending on your
class discussions and the level of your students.

For the vocabulary section of the test, choose ten of the
words from the vocabulary lists to read orally for your students.

The answers to the matching section of the test are below.

Answers to the matching section of the Advanced Short Answer Unit Test
are the same as for Short Answer Unit Test #2.

Test #1	Test #2
1. G	1. H
2. F	2. I
3. L	3. C
4. E	4. J
5. C	5. L
6. J	6. E
7. N	7. A
8. I	8. F
9. M	9. B
10. K	10. D
11. H	11. G
12. A	12. N
13. B	13. M
14. D	14. K

ADVANCED SHORT ANSWER UNIT TEST - *The Great Gatsby*

I. Matching

___ 1. Gatsby   A. Myrtle's husband

___ 2. Nick   B. "The Boarder"

___ 3. Tom   C. Daisy's husband

___ 4. Daisy   D. Nick and Jordan met him in Gatsby's library

___ 5. Jordan   E. Tom had an affair with her

___ 6. Myrtle   F. Business associate of Gatsby

___ 7. George   G. Gatsby's father

___ 8. Wolfshiem   H. Extremely wealthy man who throws extravagant parties

___ 9. Klipspringer   I. Narrator; Gatsby's neighbor

___ 10. Owl Eyes   J. The woman with whom Gatsby wants to resume a relationship

___ 11. Henry Gatz   K. Showed Gatsby how to live in the rich man's world

___ 12. James Gatz   L. Nick had a short affair with her

___ 13. Pammy   M. Daisy's little girl

___ 14. Cody   N. The Great Gatsby

Gatsby Advanced Short Answer Unit Test Page 2

II. Short Answer
1. Describe Gatsby's relationship with Daisy.

2. Compare and contrast Gatsby and Tom.

3. What is Nick's role in *Gatsby*? What does he add to the story, and how would the story have been different without him?

4. Who was responsible for Gatsby's death? Explain your choice.

5. How was Nick different from Daisy, Tom and Jordan?

6. Suppose this novel had been written from Gatsby's point of view. How would the story have changed?

Gatsby Advanced Short Answer Unit Test Page 3

III. Quotations   Explain the significance or importance of each of the following quotations:

1. "Gatsby turned out all right in the end." (Nick)

2. "I suppose she talks and -- eats, and everything." (Daisy about Pammy)

3. ". . . he stared around at his possessions in a dazed way, as though in her actual astounding presence none of it was any longer real." (Nick about Gatsby when he showed him his house)

4. "What'll we do with ourselves this afternoon?" cried Daisy, "and the day after that, and the next thirty years?"

5. "But it's so hot," insisted Daisy, . . ." and everything is so confused. Let's all go to town."

Gatsby Advanced Short Answer Unit Test Page 4

6. "You resemble the advertisement of the man," she went on innocently. (Daisy to Gatsby in front of Tom)

7. "... and it occurred to me that there was no difference between men, in intelligence or race, so profound as the difference between the sick and the well. Wilson was so sick that he looked guilty...." (Nick after the accident)

8. "They're a rotten crowd," I shouted across the lawn. "You're worth the whole damn bunch put together." (Nick to Gatsby)

9. "They were careless people, Tom and Daisy." (Nick)

10. "So we beat on, boats against the current, borne back ceaselessly into the past."

Gatsby Advanced Short Answer Unit Test Page 5

III. Vocabulary

Write down the vocabulary words you are given. Go back later and use all of those vocabulary words in a composition relating to *The Great Gatsby*.

MULTIPLE CHOICE UNIT TEST 1 - *The Great Gatsby*

I. Matching/Identify

___ 1. Gatsby   A. The Great Gatsby

___ 2. Nick   B. Daisy's little girl

___ 3. Tom   C. Nick has a short affair with her

___ 4. Daisy   D. Showed Gatsby how to live in the rich man's world

___ 5. Jordan   E. The woman with whom Gatsby wants a relationship

___ 6. Myrtle   F. Narrator; Gatsby's neighbor

___ 7. George   G. His car ran over Myrtle

___ 8. Wolfshiem   H. Gatsby's father

___ 9. Klipspringer   I. Business associate of Gatsby

___ 10. Owl Eyes   J. Tom has an affair with her

___ 11. Henry Gatz   K. Nick & Jordan meet him in Gatsby's library

___ 12. James Gatz   L. Daisy's husband

___ 13. Pammy   M. "The Boarder"

___ 14. Cody   N. Myrtle's husband

Gatsby Multiple Choice Unit Test 1 Page 2

II. Multiple Choice

1. How is Gatsby introduced into the novel?
    a. He is mentioned in a conversation between Nick and Jordan. Later Nick sees him on the lawn in the moonlight.
    b. Nick meets him at a party.
    c. Everyone talks about him at the party, but no one sees him. Later Nick sees him with Daisy.
    d. Jordan tells Daisy about Tom's affair, and Daisy meets Gatsby to begin an affair of her own to get even with Tom.

2. What are the "eyes of Dr. T. J. Eckleburg?
    a. Seeing eye dogs that the doctor trains for the Association for the Blind
    b. A group of security guards who monitor the doctor's home and offices
    c. A new kind of contact lens that the doctor has just developed
    d. An illustration on a billboard

3. What reason did Myrtle give for marrying George Wilson?
    a. She had to do something to get away from her abusive parents.
    b. She did it to spite George's former girlfriend.
    c. She thought he was a gentleman; later she found out differently.
    d. She didn't think she would ever find a husband, and she was grateful to him for asking her.

4. What did Tom do to Myrtle when she mentioned Daisy's name?
    a. He hit her and broke her nose.
    b. He laughed and called her a jealous fool.
    c. He taunted her and repeated Daisy's name several more times.
    d. He ignored her and went on with his conversation with Nick.

5. What kind of people come to Gatsby's parties?
    a. The newly rich, famous, and their friends
    b. Only the residents of West Egg
    c. Scholars and intellectuals from area universities
    d. Mostly Gatsby's business associates

6. What had the green light on the dock meant to Gatsby?
    a. It was clear to land the hydroplane.
    b. It was safe for him and his guests to go swimming.
    c. It stood for his vision of his future with Daisy.
    d. It was a tribute to his companions who had died in the war.

Gatsby Multiple Choice Unit Test 1 Page 3

7. What is Daisy's opinion of Gatsby's party and how does it affect him?
    a. She likes it immensely. He is so pleased that he asks her to help him arrange his next party.
    b. She doesn't like it. He becomes angry and vows never to see her again.
    c. She doesn't like it. He becomes depressed.
    d. She likes it somewhat. He asks her to attend several more before she gives him her opinion.

8. Why do the four drive into the city on such a hot afternoon?
    a. They have tickets for a Broadway matinee.
    b. Gatsby offers to take them out in the ocean on his yacht.
    c. Nick knows of a hotel that specializes in icy cold baths.
    d. Daisy wants to avoid confrontation and get away from her problems.

9. What happens on the way home from New York?
    a. Nick and Jordan get into an argument and Nick says he will take the train home.
    b. Tom realizes he loves Daisy, and stops at the garage to end his affair with Myrtle.
    c. Gatsby is speeding, is stopped by the police and is arrested for drunk driving.
    d. Daisy is driving Gatsby's car. She hits Myrtle Wilson, but keeps driving.

10. Which of these statements about other characters' reactions to Myrtle's death is true?
    a. Wilson thinks she deserved it for cheating on him.
    b. Tom's first instinct is to protect himself. Later he cries.
    c. Nick is not interested because he hardly knows her.
    d. Gatsby thinks he can make up for it by paying Wilson a lot of money.

11. Why does Wilson believe that Gatsby killed Myrtle?
    a. An eyewitness identified the car and the driver.
    b. He traces the license number and finds it is Gatsby's.
    c. A mechanic friend gives him the tip.
    d. Tom tells him that the car is Gatsby's.

12. Why is the book that Gatsby's father shows Nick important to the novel?
    a. It is a book that Daisy once gave him, and shows that she did love him.
    b. It foreshadows Gatsby's death.
    c. It shows Gatsby's romantic spirit and desire to get ahead.
    d. It is the only memorabilia the father has, and symbolizes his relationship with his son.

Gatsby Multiple Choice Unit Test 1 Page 4

III. Composition

F. Scott Fitzgerald wrote *The Great Gatsby* in 1925, and here we are reading it so many years later. Why? What makes this book a "classic"?

Gatsby Multiple Choice Unit Test 1 Page 5

IV. Vocabulary

___ 1. Pandered	a. a long motor vehicle for passengers
___ 2. Corrugated	b. to strengthen or support with other evidence
___ 3. Addenda	c. relating to air or other gases
___ 4. Nebulous	d. to act as a go-between in sexual intrigues
___ 5. Caterwauling	e. shrill, discordant sound
___ 6. Denizen	f. an inhabitant
___ 7. Expostulation	g. a small brook or stream
___ 8. Contiguous	h. a container that holds items or matter
___ 9. Caravansary	i. close observation
___10. Contingency	j. to shape into folds or parallel ridges and grooves
___11. Omnibus	k. to dissuade or correct
___12. Scrutiny	l. a deceptive stratagem or device
___13. Pneumatic	m. cloudy, misty or hazy
___14. Rivulets	n. something added especially a supplement to a book
___15. Inexplicable	o. to travel or pass across
___16. Traversed	p. something incidental to something else
___17. Subterfuges	q. difficult to explain
___18. Meretricious	r. attracting attention in a vulgar manner
___19. Corroborate	s. connecting without a break
___20. Receptacles	t. a large inn

MULTIPLE CHOICE UNIT TEST 2 - *The Great Gatsby*

I. Matching

___ 1. Gatsby   A. Myrtle's husband

___ 2. Nick   B. "The Boarder"

___ 3. Tom   C. Daisy's husband

___ 4. Daisy   D. Nick and Jordan met him in Gatsby's library

___ 5. Jordan   E. Tom had an affair with her

___ 6. Myrtle   F. Business associate of Gatsby

___ 7. George   G. Gatsby's father

___ 8. Wolfshiem   H. Extremely wealthy man who throws extravagant parties

___ 9. Klipspringer   I. Narrator; Gatsby's neighbor

___ 10. Owl Eyes   J. The woman with whom Gatsby wants to resume a relationship

___ 11. Henry Gatz   K. Showed Gatsby how to live in the rich man's world

___ 12. James Gatz   L. Nick had a short affair with her

___ 13. Pammy   M. Daisy's little girl

___ 14. Cody   N. The Great Gatsby

Gatsby Multiple Choice Unit Test 2 Page 2

II. Multiple Choice

1. How does the narrator describe Gatsby?
    a. Gatsby was brilliant, although somewhat smug and self-centered.
    b. Gatsby had an extraordinary gift for hope, and a romantic readiness.
    c. Gatsby was a big, hulking brute of a man.
    d. Gatsby was self-assured and showed an almost boundless enthusiasm about most topics.

2. How does Nick know Daisy and Tom?
    a. Nick and Tom served in the war together. He met Daisy at their wedding.
    b. Nick and Daisy went to school together. Daisy was dating Tom.
    c. He met them through a friend of his parents in Chicago.
    d. Daisy and Nick are cousins. Nick and Tom knew each other from school.

3. What kind of person is Daisy?
    a. Daisy is flighty and very superficial.
    b. Daisy is an intellectual.
    c. Daisy is a down-to-earth, sweet, naive young woman.
    d. Daisy is just plain mean.

4. What are the "eyes of Dr. T. J. Eckleburg"?
    a. Seeing eye dogs that the doctor trains for the Association for the Blind
    b. A group of security guards who monitor the doctor's home and offices
    c. A new kind of contact lens that the doctor has just developed
    d. An illustration on a billboard

5. Which one of these does not represent Gatsby's wealth
    a. Made in the post-war period
    b. Spending on flashy, extravagant things
    c. Old, family money
    d. Wild parties

6. Which is not one of the stories about Gatsby?
    a. He inherited his money from his mother, a French baroness.
    b. He killed a man.
    c. He was a German spy during the war.
    d. He was in the American army during the war.

Gatsby Multiple Choice Unit Test 2 Page 3

7. What does Jordan tell Nick about Daisy, Gatsby and Tom?
    a. They all grew up together in Louisiana. Tom and Gatsby had been best friends until their jealousy about Daisy got between them. Tom doesn't know that Gatsby lives nearby. Gatsby wants to make sure Nick never invites Daisy and Tom to one of the parties.
    b. Gatsby knows Tom through business dealings. He met Daisy recently at a party and wanted to get to know her better.
    c. Daisy and Gatsby had had an earlier romance. Her parents wouldn't let her see him off to war. Then she married Tom, and soon found out that he had a mistress.
    d. Gatsby and Daisy have been seeing each other for a long time. Gatsby offered Tom a large sum of money to divorce Daisy, but Tom refused.

8. What had the green light on the dock meant to Gatsby?
    a. It was clear to land the hydroplane.
    b. It was safe for him and his guests to go swimming.
    c. It stood for his vision of his future with Daisy.
    d. It was a tribute to his companions who had died in the war.

9. What happens on the way home from New York?
    a. Nick and Jordan get into an argument and Nick says he will take the train home.
    b. Tom realizes he loves Daisy, and stops at the garage to end his affair with Myrtle.
    c. Gatsby is speeding, is stopped by the police and is arrested for drunk driving.
    d. Daisy is driving Gatsby's car. She hits Myrtle Wilson, but keeps driving.

10. What does Michaelis believe caused Myrtle to run?
    a. She was drunk and didn't know what she was doing.
    b. She saw Tom in the yellow car and was running to him.
    c. She was running away from her husband.
    d. She was trying to make it to the train station on time.

11. Why does Wilson believe that Gatsby killed Myrtle?
    a. An eyewitness identified the car and the driver.
    b. He traces the license number and finds it is Gatsby's.
    c. A mechanic friend gives him the tip.
    d. Tom tells him that the car is Gatsby's.

12. What does Wilson do?
    a. He goes to the police.
    b. He kills Gatsby and himself.
    c. He leaves the city, a defeated man.
    d. He hires a thug to kill Gatsby and destroy the car.

Gatsby Multiple Choice Unit Test 2 Page 4

III. Composition

    What is the point of *The Great Gatsby*? When we read books, we usually come away from our reading experience a little richer, having given more thought to a particular aspect of life. What do you think F. Scott Fitzgerald intended us to gain from reading his novel?

Gatsby Multiple Choice Unit Test 2 Page 5

IV. Vocabulary

___ 1. Obstetrical   a. suggestive

___ 2. Euphemisms   b. an intricate structure of interconnecting passages

___ 3. Denizen   c. a long motor vehicle for passengers

___ 4. Nebulous   d. lacking definite form

___ 5. Amorphous   e. unable to think in a clear or orderly manner

___ 6. Erroneous   f. feeling or showing haughty disdain

___ 7. Libertine   g. a prince or chief

___ 8. Hauteur   h. a short, witty poem

___ 9. Redolent   i. haughtiness in bearing and attitude

___10. Labyrinth   j. the act of substituting a mild indirect term for a harsh, blunt or offensive one

___11. Supercilious   k. something added especially a supplement to a book

___12. Epigram   l. cloudy, misty or hazy

___13. Rivulets   m. to walk in a sleeplike condition

___14. Incoherent   n. a large inn

___15. Inexplicable   o. care of a pregnant woman

___16. Omnibus   p. difficult to explain

___17. Somnambulatory   q. one who acts without moral restraint

___18. Rajah   r. mistaken

___19. Addenda   s. an inhabitant

___20. Caravansary   t. a small brook or stream

ANSWER SHEET - *The Great Gatsby*
Multiple Choice Unit Tests

I. Matching
1. ___
2. ___
3. ___
4. ___
5. ___
6. ___
7. ___
8. ___
9. ___
10. ___
11. ___
12. ___
13. ___
14. ___

II. Multiple Choice
1. ___
2. ___
3. ___
4. ___
5. ___
6. ___
7. ___
8. ___
9. ___
10. ___
11. ___
12. ___

IV. Vocabulary
1. ___
2. ___
3. ___
4. ___
5. ___
6. ___
7. ___
8. ___
9. ___
10. ___
11. ___
12. ___
13. ___
14. ___
15. ___
16. ___
17. ___
18. ___
19. ___
20. ___

ANSWER KEY: MULTIPLE CHOICE UNIT TESTS - *The Great Gatsby*

Answers to Unit Test 1 are in the left column. Answers to Unit Test 2 are in the right column.

I. Matching	II. Multiple Choice	IV. Vocabulary
1. G H	1. A B	1. D O
2. F I	2. D D	2. J J
3. L C	3. C A	3. N S
4. E J	4. A D	4. M L
5. C L	5. A C	5. E D
6. J E	6. C A	6. F R
7. N A	7. C C	7. K Q
8. I F	8. D C	8. S I
9. M B	9. D D	9. T A
10. K D	10. B C	10. P B
11. H G	11. D D	11. A F
12. A N	12. C B	12. I H
13. B M		13. C T
14. D K		14. G E
		15. Q P
		16. O C
		17. L M
		18. R G
		19. B K
		20. H N

UNIT RESOURCE MATERIALS

BULLETIN BOARD IDEAS - *The Great Gatsby*

1. Save one corner of the board for the best of students' *The Great Gatsby* writing assignments.

2. Make a "Lifestyles of the Rich and Famous" bulletin board showing people who are wealthy in our society. Have students each research one rich and famous person, find a picture of him/her, and write a short biography of the person. Put students' work up on the bulletin board.

3. Do a "Miss Manners Says" bulletin board on which you include rules of etiquette.

4. Take one of the word search puzzles from the extra activities packet and with a marker copy it over in a large size on the bulletinboard. Write the clue words to find to one side. Invite students prior to and after class to find the words and circle them on the bulletinboard.

5. Write several of the most significant quotations from the book onto the board on brightly colored paper.

6. Make a bulletin board listing the vocabulary words for this unit. As you complete sections of the novel and discuss the vocabulary for each section, write the definitions on the bulletin board. (If your board is one students face frequently, it will help them learn the words.)

7. Do a bulletin board about career planning and tips for success.

8. Find pictures of various homes which represent the styles of the homes mentioned in the novel. Title the board: *The Great Gatsby* HOME IS WHERE THE HEART IS. Identify each style home with the appropriate characters.

EXTRA ACTIVITIES - *The Great Gatsby*

One of the difficulties in teaching a novel is that all students don't read at the same speed. One student who likes to read may take the book home and finish it in a day or two. Sometimes a few students finish the in-class assignments early. The problem, then, is finding suitable extra activities for students.

One thing that helps is to keep a little library in the classroom. For this unit on *The Great Gatsby*, you might check out from the school library other related books and articles about the Roaring Twenties, life among the currently rich and famous, guides with tips for success in life and business, financial planning guides, books about career possibilities, etc. A biography about Fitzgerald and other books written by him would also be appropriate.

Other things you may keep on hand are puzzles. We have made some relating directly to *The Great Gatsby* for you. Feel free to duplicate them.

Some students may like to draw. You might devise a contest or allow some extra-credit grade for students who draw characters or scenes from *The Great Gatsby*. Note, too, that if the students do not want to keep their drawings you may pick up some extra bulletin board materials this way. If you have a contest and you supply the prize (a CD or something like that perhaps), you could, possibly, make the drawing itself a non-refundable entry fee.

The pages which follow contain games, puzzles and worksheets. The keys, when appropriate, follow the puzzle or worksheet. There are two main groups of activities: one group for the unit; that is, generally relating to the *Great Gatsby* text, and another group of activities related strictly to the *Great Gatsby* vocabulary.

Directions for these games, puzzles and worksheets are self-explanatory. The object here is to provide you with extra materials you may use in any way you choose.

MORE ACTIVITIES - *The Great Gatsby*

1. Pick a chapter or scene with a great deal of dialogue and have the students act it out on a stage. (Perhaps you could assign various scenes to different groups of students so more than one scene could be acted and more students could participate.)

2. As an introductory activity, create a "Lifestyles of the Rich and Famous" bulletin board showing people who are wealthy in our society. Have students each research one rich and famous person, find a picture of him/her, and write a short biography of the person. Put students' work up on the bulletinboard.

3. The songs in *Gatsby* relate directly to the times in which they were popular. Have students choose two currently popular songs they think best represent current times, and explain why they think those particular songs are appropriate.

4. Have students design a book cover (front and back and inside flaps) for *The Great Gatsby*.

5. Have students design a bulletin board (ready to be put up; not just sketched) for *The Great Gatsby*.

6. Have students write a plot summary of the novel supposing that Daisy had not run over Myrtle.

7. Compare and contrast prohibition in the 1920's with the anti-drug and anti-alcohol movements in the 1980's and 1990's.

8. Have students rewrite a plot summary using Gatsby's point of view.

9. Have a mini-unit about how to be successful. First have students define "success." Then, through speakers, videos, research and/or discussion, examine the many different things people can do for themselves to become successful.

WORD SEARCH - *The Great Gatsby*

All words in this list are associated with *The Great Gatsby*. The words are placed backwards, forward, diagonally, up and down. The included words are listed below the word searches.

```
D M D D G H Z K M N E L T R Y M C A R E L E S S
Q R C C K S T O G J I O T M T S D A V A G R G H
T N Y K E L O S Y S W C M Z O V I A R F C G K N
C A T H E R I N E N F A K X E X E A G R E E N D
W O S F E E E M O W P I P R R L F E D Y A A B J
J A D C H N A G N I D V T A Z Q O O E N D W T N
Q B I Y O J R Z N X S I L Z R R M S R R W Z A P
D O G N D U Q Y P I S N M N G T O M O D P N G Y
Q X J P V J S Z K E R O A E O E M J G G Q N S J
C P R D L I N I M C N P S M P S R E L Z I Z J E
B O A T S U T E N E Y B S T A G E A N K N D L F
L W W R W L N E Y Y N J B P F W R X L T Q U G H
V V V L T T V C J Q Y H Q B I E G U V D D B J K
J T S F E I J B H N Q C N V N L H Q R E B C V T
B G C W D Y E P S E H M P U T M K S H H J J X P
P V Z Z P M E S X H O V F C P P B C M H J J Y L
V L L W L L K S T P M N W O L F S H I E M L C L
```

ADVERTISEMENT	DOG	JAMES	NICK
APARTMENT	EGG	JORDAN	NOSE
ASHES	EYES	KLIPSPRINGER	OWLEYES
BOATS	FITZGERALD	LEAVE	OXFORD
CAR	FUNERAL	LUNCHEON	PAMMY
CARELESS	GATSBY	MANSION	PARTIES
CARRAWAY	GEORGE	MCKEE	ROOM
CATHERINE	GREEN	MIDWEST	SCHEDULE
CODY	HENRY	MONEY	TOM
COUSIN	HULKING	MYRTLE	TOWN
DAISY	INVITE	ND	WOLFSHIEM

CROSSWORD - *The Great Gatsby*

CROSSWORD CLUES - *The Great Gatsby*

Across
4. Gatsby loves her
6. Tries to impress and rekindle a relationship with Daisy
10. Few people attended Gatsby's
13. East or West _____
14. Wilson locked Myrtle in her ____
15. It was at 158th Street
16. _____ of Dr. T.J. Eckleburg
17. Tom broke Myrtle's
18. Mr. Gatz; Gatsby's father
20. Gatsby throws grand ones for entertainment
22. Gatsby's real name
23. Tells Nick Gatsby is related to Kaiser Wilhelm
24. Home area of the narrator
25. You resemble the _____ of the man.
28. Showed Gatsby how to live in the rich man's world
29. Gatsby had Jordan discuss this matter with Nick
30. It took Gatsby three years to make the money to buy this
31. Miss Baker; Daisy's friend
32. Nick's relationship to Daisy
33. Tom's mistress

Down
1. Daisy and Tom are _____ people
2. Ask to come to a party
3. Color of the light on the dock
4. What Mrs. Wilson bought while out with Tom and Nick
5. It was in the Hopalong Cassidy book
6. Myrtle's husband
7. Daisy's husband
8. So we beat on, _____ against the current ....
9. Myrtle's sister
10. Author
11. Gatsby wants Daisy to _____ Tom
12. Daisy runs into Myrtle with Gatsby's
17. Initials of Gatsby's home state
19. Narrator; Gatsby's neighbor
20. Daisy's little girl
21. Gatsby told Nick he was educated there
25. Valley of _____; industrial zone
26. Everything's so confused; let's all go to ____
27. Her voice is full of _____

CROSSWORD ANSWER KEY - *The Great Gatsby*

MATCHING QUIZ/WORKSHEET 1 - *The Great Gatsby*

___ 1. JORDAN   A. Miss Baker; Daisy's friend

___ 2. GATSBY   B. Gatsby's real name

___ 3. MONEY   C. You resemble the _____ of the man.

___ 4. TOWN   D. The boarder

___ 5. GREEN   E. Wilson locked Myrtle in her _____

___ 6. GEORGE   F. Business associate of Gatsby

___ 7. TOM   G. Color of the light on the dock

___ 8. WOLFSHIEM   H. Gatsby throws grand ones for entertainment

___ 9. BOATS   I. Myrtle's husband

___ 10. ADVERTISEMENT   J. Everything's so confused, let's all go to _____

___ 11. EGG   K. Tom broke Myrtle's

___ 12. CARELESS   L. Daisy's husband

___ 13. PARTIES   M. East or West _____

___ 14. FITZGERALD   N. Daisy and Tom are _____ people

___ 15. JAMES   O. Nick's last name

___ 16. CARRAWAY   P. Tries to impress and rekindle a relationship with Daisy

___ 17. OXFORD   Q. So we beat on, _____ against the current ....

___ 18. KLIPSPRINGER   R. Author

___ 19. NOSE   S. Gatsby told Nick he was educated there

___ 20. ROOM   T. Her voice is full of _____

MATCHING QUIZ/WORKSHEET 2 - *The Great Gatsby*

___ 1. KLIPSPRINGER   A. The boarder

___ 2. OXFORD   B. Miss Baker; Daisy's friend

___ 3. BOATS   C. Her voice is full of _____

___ 4. INVITE   D. Gatsby loves her

___ 5. HULKING   E. _____ of Dr. T.J. Eckleburg

___ 6. PARTIES   F. Daisy's little girl

___ 7. SCHEDULE   G. Gatsby throws grand ones for entertainment

___ 8. WOLFSHIEM   H. It was in the Hopalong Cassidy book

___ 9. JORDAN   I. So we beat on, _____ against the current ....

___ 10. FITZGERALD   J. Daisy's husband

___ 11. GREEN   K. Author

___ 12. DAISY   L. Wilson locked Myrtle in her _____

___ 13. MONEY   M. Color of the light on the dock

___ 14. PAMMY   N. What Mrs. Wilson bought while out with Tom and Nick

___ 15. TOM   O. Home area of the narrator

___ 16. MIDWEST   P. Ask to come to a party

___ 17. ROOM   Q. Gatsby told Nick he was educated there

___ 18. JAMES   R. Tom hates that word - even in kidding

___ 19. DOG   S. Business associate of Gatsby

___ 20. EYES   T. Gatsby's real name

KEY: MATCHING QUIZ/WORKSHEETS - *The Great Gatsby*

Worksheet 1	Worksheet 2
1. A	1. A
2. P	2. Q
3. T	3. I
4. J	4. P
5. G	5. R
6. I	6. G
7. L	7. H
8. F	8. S
9. Q	9. B
10. C	10. K
11. M	11. M
12. N	12. D
13. H	13. C
14. R	14. F
15. B	15. J
16. O	16. O
17. S	17. L
18. D	18. T
19. K	19. N
20. E	20. E

JUGGLE LETTER REVIEW GAME CLUE SHEET - *The Great Gatsby*

SCRAMBLED	WORD	CLUE
SSAHE	ASHES	Valley of _____; industrial zone
INNASMO	MANSION	It took Gatsby three years to make the money to buy this
NLRFEUA	FUNERAL	Few people attended Gatsby's
CMEEK	MCKEE	Tell Nick Gatsby is related to Kaiser Wilhelm
NVTIEI	INVITE	Ask to come to a party
ONES	NOSE	Tom broke Myrtle's
EHSMIFWOL	WOLFSHIEM	Business associate of Gatsby
AYSGTB	GATSBY	Tries to impress and rekindle a relationship with Daisy
MSEAJ	JAMES	Gatsby's real name
SATOB	BOATS	So we beat one, _____ against the current ....
CNNHOULE	LUNCHEON	Gatsby had Jordan discuss this matter with Nick
YMAPM	PAMMY	Daisy's little girl
ODYC	CODY	Showed Gatsby how to live in the rich man's world
LEMYTR	MYRTLE	Tom's mistress
WSEOLYE	OWLEYES	Nick met him in the library; he went to Gatsby's funeral
WARARYAC	CARRAWAY	Nick's last name
EGEGRO	GEORGE	Myrtle's husband
IPGKRESNRLIP	KLIPSPRINGER	The boarder
OGD	DOG	What Mrs. Wilson bought while out with Tom and Nick
ELEAV	LEAVE	Gatsby wants Daisy to _____ Tom
ICOUNS	COUSIN	Nick's relationship to Daisy
NTIECAREH	CATHERINE	Myrtle's sister
SEECSRLA	CARELESS	Daisy and Tom are _____ people
GGE	EGG	East or West _____
TRPSAIE	PARTIES	Gatsby throws grand ones for entertainment
RCA	CAR	Daisy runs into Myrtle with Gatsby's
EESY	EYES	_____ of Dr. T.J. Eckleburg
EMWISTD	MIDWEST	Home area of the narrator
OWNT	TOWN	Everything's so confused, let's all go to _____
DN	ND	Initials of Gatsby's home state
IHNLGKU	HULKING	Tom hates that word - even in kidding
AGZTIDELRF	FITZGERALD	Author
OFXODR	OXFORD	Gatsby told Nick he was educated there
ORMO	ROOM	Wilson locked Myrtle in her _____

VOCABULARY RESOURCE MATERIALS

VOCABULARY WORD SEARCH - *The Great Gatsby*

All words in this list are associated with *The Great Gatsby* with an emphasis on the vocabulary words chosen for study in the text. The words are placed backwards, forward, diagonally, up and down. The included words are listed below.

```
H M Q L X W Z L A Z P S F R M E S T K X J W Z H
H S S H M L N P H D L Q U H N Z R Y M D D K X Y
A F F E C T A T I O N S R O T O G R A V U R E M
E N W N G N G I X R D E Z E U N S R O L D P P J
M U D D D U G U C T S E D C C G I C A N K W W W
X E P E T R F I N N U E N D O E I Y R J E R X X
Q S R H T N E R L P I E X I A R P T R U A O D D
P E C E E A K D E A U V X P Z W R T N B T H U N
D X S O T M G N O T C N O T O E S O A O A I T S
R P R U N R I U B L B I C R E S N H B C C L N K
O X N K P V I S R W E U R T P M T I R O L B H Y
Y M Y E V E I C M R T N S T U N P U T K R E F J
G Z N V U M R V I S O E T U E A E O L R V A S B
T T L I W M F C I O T C P Z O T L B R A E P T L
K S C Y B M A L I A U E S I U H S R U I T B Y E
G Y B C H U U T D L L S L A G S P B L L Z I I F
P R Q Z T C S Q I P I B H U B R J R O Z O I O L
T K K X O X C J B C T O M W V R A S O R G U N N
T F V B S L H V M X C L U J V I N M F M V F S G
T R A V E R S E D J B M Y S F K R L S J A G K W
```

ADDENDA	ERRONEOUS	NEBULOUS	REDOLENT
AFFECTATIONS	EUPHEMISMS	OBSTETRICAL	RIVULETS
AMORPHOUS	EXPOSTULATION	OCULIST	ROTOGRAVURE
CONTIGUOUS	EXTEMPORIZING	OMNIBUS	SCRUTINY
CONVIVIAL	HAUTEUR	PANDERED	SUBTERFUGES
CORROBORATE	INNUENDO	PNEUMATIC	SUPERCILIOUS
CORRUGATED	LABYRINTH	PROVINCIAL	TRAVERSED
DENIZEN	LIBERTINE	RAJAH	UNPUNCTUAL
EPIGRAM	MERETRICIOUS	RECEPTACLES	

VOCABULARY CROSSWORD - *The Great Gatsby*

Across
1. a large inn
6. something added especially a supplement to a book
9. to shape into folds or parallel ridges and grooves
13. an indirect usually derogatory implication in expression
16. haughtiness in bearing and attitude
17. a long motor vehicle for passengers
18. a physician who treats diseases of the eyes
19. suggestive
20. merry; festive
21. possibility

Down
1. adjacent; sharing an edge
2. lacking definite form
3. close observation
4. a prince or chief
5. corresponding in size or degree
6. a show, pretense or display
7. an inhabitant
8. to act as a go-between in sexual intrigues
9. shrill, discordant sound
10. a short, witty poem
11. to strengthen or support with other evidence
12. unable to think in a clear or orderly manner
14. a small brook or stream
15. mistaken

VOCABULARY CROSSWORD ANSWER KEY - *The Great Gatsby*

VOCABULARY WORKSHEET 1 - *The Great Gatsby*

___ 1. Teetered   A. Settlement of differences in which concessions are made

___ 2. Irrelevant   B. Oppressed; ill-treated and harassed

___ 3. Compensation   C. Not likely

___ 4. Fraud   D. To come forth from something

___ 5. Obscure   E. Native

___ 6. Unanimous   F. People who say they believe one thing but actually believe in the opposite

___ 7. Predicament   G. Extreme harshness; rigor

___ 8. Hypocrite   H. Deliberate deception for unfair or unlawful gain

___ 9. Indigenous   I. Authoritative statements

___ 10. Dispelled   J. Unaware

___ 11. Prejudice   K. Swayed back and forth with a seesaw motion

___ 12. Improbable   L. Things that cause trouble, lack of ease or difficulty

___ 13. Inconveniences   M. The condition of being puzzled

___ 14. Pronouncements   N. Not applicable; having nothing to do with the matter at hand

___ 15. Compromise   O. Preconceived preference or idea; bias

___ 16. Tyranny   P. Inconspicuous; undistinguished; not well-known

___ 17. Emerge   Q. To have done away with

___ 18. Persecuted   R. Troublesome situation

___ 19. Perplexity   S. In complete agreement

___ 20. Oblivious   T. Something given or received as substitution or payment

VOCABULARY WORKSHEET 2 - *The Great Gatsby*

___ 1. Pronouncements   A. Obtained

___ 2. Predicament   B. To keep in existence; maintain; prolong

___ 3. Ecclesiastical   C. Deliberate deception for unfair or unlawful gain

___ 4. Teetered   D. Without sophistication; artless; innocent

___ 5. Chameleon   E. Poor person

___ 6. Ingenuous   F. Authoritative statements

___ 7. Inaudible   G. Bring one's self down to an inferior level

___ 8. Dispelled   H. Unable to be heard

___ 9. Quibbling   I. To envy the possession or enjoyment of something

___ 10. Acquired   J. To have done away with

___ 11. Condescended   K. Act of avoiding

___ 12. Antagonize   L. In a self-satisfied manner

___ 13. Sustain   M. Incur the dislike of someone; counteract

___ 14. Adjacent   N. Pertaining to the church

___ 15. Unanimous   O. Close to; next to

___ 16. Pauper   P. Changeable person

___ 17. Fraud   Q. In complete agreement

___ 18. Evasion   R. Swayed back and forth in a seesaw motion

___ 19. Complacently   S. Making petty distinctions or irrelevant observations

___ 20. Begrudge   T. Troublesome situation

KEY: VOCABULARY WORKSHEETS - *The Great Gatsby*

Worksheet 1	Worksheet 2
1. K	1. F
2. N	2. T
3. T	3. N
4. H	4. R
5. P	5. P
6. S	6. D
7. R	7. H
8. F	8. J
9. E	9. S
10. Q	10. A
11. O	11. G
12. C	12. M
13. L	13. B
14. I	14. O
15. A	15. Q
16. G	16. E
17. D	17. C
18. B	18. K
19. M	19. L
20. J	20. I

VOCABULARY JUGGLE LETTER REVIEW GAME CLUES - *The Great Gatsby*

SCRAMBLED	WORD	CLUE
IHRNLTABY	LABYRINTH	an intricate structure of interconnecting passages
UPIACTMNE	PNEUMATIC	relating to air or other gases
NIICVLAOV	CONVIVIAL	merry; festive
MOPERPRYTE	PREEMPTORY	to take the place of
OSIRRMEUTCEI	MERETRICIOUS	attracting attention in a vulgar manner
DADDENA	ADDENDA	something added especially a supplement to a book
IXLCLAENPIBE	INEXPLICABLE	difficult to explain
TOLSAPTIOXENU	EXPOSTULATION	to dissuade or correct
ARHJA	RAJAH	a prince or chief
REDEARTVS	TRAVERSED	to travel or pass across
TOAAICFSNFTE	AFFECTATIONS	a show, pretense or display
ETRBSUSEFUG	SUBTERFUGES	a deceptive stratagem or device
UURHTEA	HAUTEUR	haughtiness in bearing and attitude
EDNZINE	DENIZEN	an inhabitant
ERTLBNIIE	LIBERTINE	one who acts without moral restraint
PGRAMIE	EPIGRAM	a short, witty poem
DERDPEAN	PANDERED	acted as a go-between in sexual intrigues
TSCECERAEPL	RECEPTACLES	a container that holds items or matter
OSUITOGUCN	CONTIGUOUS	adjacent; sharing an edge
ISEUCRLOUISP	SUPERCILIOUS	feeling or showing haughty disdain
IERCOSTLBTA	OBSTETRICAL	care of a pregnant woman
RRTOCEDUAG	CORRUGATED	to shape into folds or parallel ridges and grooves
UNLEUSBO	NEBULOUS	cloudy, misty or hazy
CHIEERNNTO	INCOHERENT	unable to think in a clear or orderly manner
OCINYENTGNC	CONTINGENCY	possibility
UISMMSPEERH	EUPHEMISMS	a mild indirect term substituted for a harsh, blunt or offensive one
RSCVARAANYA	CARAVANSARY	a large inn
URGAVROETRO	ROTOGRAVURE	printed material, such as a newspaper
NODNNIUE	INNUENDO	an indirect usually derogative implication in expression
ODETENRL	REDOLENT	suggestive
MUOPOASRH	AMORPHOUS	lacking definite form
EIIZNRMPGXEOT	EXTEMPORIZING	to perform without prior preparation
BOUNSMI	OMNIBUS	a long motor vehicle for passengers